MW00668059

The Aleutians Campaign

The Official Navy History of the Only World War Two Invasion of US Soil

Red and Black Publishers, St Petersburg, Florida

Originally written 1943, published by Naval Historical Center, Department Of The Navy, Washington DC, 1993

Library of Congress Cataloging-in-Publication Data

The Aleutians campaign : the official Navy history of the only World War Two invasion of US soil.
    p. cm.
  "Originally written 1943, published by Naval Historical Center, Department Of The Navy, Washington DC, 1993"--T.p. verso.
    ISBN 978-1-934941-88-1
1. World War, 1939-1945--Campaigns--Alaska--Aleutian Islands.
    D769.87.A4A44 2010
    940.54'28--dc22

                                     2010015083

Red and Black Publishers, PO Box 7542, St Petersburg, Florida, 33734
Contact us at: info@RedandBlackPublishers.com
    Printed and manufactured in the United States of America

Contents

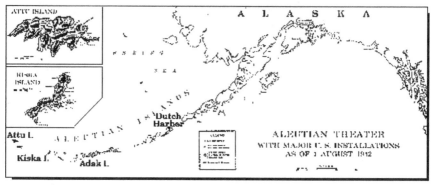

ALEUTIAN THEATER
WITH MAJOR U. S. INSTALLATIONS
AS OF 1 AUGUST 1942

ATTU ISLAND

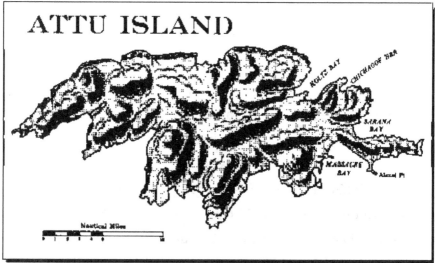

Nautical Miles

KISKA ISLAND

Nautical Miles

Introduction

Until the end of the Pacific War no one can make a conclusive statement of the objectives of the Japanese attack on the Aleutian Islands in June 1942. The enemy may have been planning the subsequent conquest of all the islands in order to obtain access to Canada and our northwestern states. He may even have aimed at an immediate invasion of Alaska, only to be deterred by our victory at Midway. It is well known that the Japanese had long coveted Alaska and the Aleutians, and that many of their military leaders considered these poorly defended outposts the logical route for an invasion of North America.

The enemy's intentions may have been less ambitious, however. He may merely have planned to protect his northern flank, to divide our forces, and to complicate our defense of Hawaii and the West Coast after the expected capture of Midway.

Whatever his primary motives, the crushing blow administered by our forces in the mid-Pacific drastically revised the strategic situation. The reasons why Japan clung thereafter to her footholds in the western Aleutians are obscure. But it is probable that Attu and Kiska were either to provide jumping-off places for a future invasion, or to constitute advanced observation posts and defenses for the Empire. Perhaps both ends were envisaged. At all events, it was immediately clear that the occupation provided a continuing threat to our security. Even if this threat did not develop, any plans for seizing the offensive in the Central Pacific would be difficult to execute while the enemy maintained his flanking positions in the north. Furthermore, considering the war as a whole, every day that hostile troops remained on American soil was as beneficial to Japanese morale as it was deleterious to that of our own people.

The situation was grave. Because of our commitments elsewhere, the means of quickly resolving it were far from adequate. As a result, the Japanese were ejected from the Aleutians only after 15 months of arduous operations which were hampered by shortages afloat, ashore, and in the air, as well as by almost insuperable obstacles of weather and terrain.

The Geographical Factor

One cannot form an accurate picture of the Aleutians Campaign without a thorough understanding of the geographical and meteorological peculiarities of the area. Practically every offensive or defensive move by either side was conditioned as much by terrain and weather as by the efforts of the enemy.

Approximately 120 islands comprise the Aleutian chain, which stretches from the tip of the Alaskan peninsula to within 90 miles of Kamchatka. The easternmost island, Unimak, is also the largest, measuring 65 by 22 miles. To the southwest is Unalaska, on the north coast of which Dutch Harbor is located. Unalaska is about 2,000 miles from both San Francisco and Honolulu. Westward, in order, lie Umnak, Atka, and Adak. Kiska is 610 miles west of Dutch Harbor, while Attu, the westernmost American island, is nearly 1,000 miles from the Alaskan mainland and 750 miles northeast of the northernmost of the Japanese Kurile Islands. Attu is about 20 by 35 miles in size.

Terrain

All the Aleutians are volcanic in origin. They are uniformly rocky and barren, with precipitous mountains and scant vegetation. The mountains are conical in shape and covered with volcanic ash and resembling cinders. There are no trees on the islands, except a few stunted spruces at Dutch Harbor, and no brush, which complicates the building and heating problems. The lowlands are blanketed with tundra or muskeg as much as three feet thick. This growth forms a spongy carpet which makes walking most difficult. Below the tundra is volcanic ash which has been finely ground and watersoaked until it has the consistency of slime. In many places water is trapped in ponds under the tundra. Frequently men have fallen into these bogs and been lost.

Throughout the Aleutians, jagged shorelines and submerged rock formations render navigation hazardous. Conditions are least unfavorable in the eastern islands. Unalaska has two comparatively good anchorages, Dutch Harbor and Captain's Bay, while Umnak has three, of which Nikolski Bay on the west coast is the most important. Farther west, protected anchorages are scarce. Atka has two fair harbors. Adak has three small bays on the west coast. Amchitka offers one small bay on the east coast. Neither Kiska nor Attu possesses a harbor which is entirely suitable for larger vessels. Kiska is the better endowed, having a broad, moderately deep indentation on the eastern shore which is protected by Little Kiska Island, lying across its mouth. Attu has four less adequately guarded bays—Holtz, Chichagof, and Sarana on the northeast side, and Massacre Bay on the southeast. Of these Chichagof is the best.

Weather

Meteorological conditions become progressively worse as the western end of the island chain is approached. On Attu five or six days a week are likely to be rainy, and there are hardly more than eight or ten clear days a year. The rest of the time, even if rain is not falling, fog of varying density is the rule rather than the exception. Weather is highly localized, however, and areas of high visibility will often be found within 20 miles of fog concentration.

Throughout the islands annual rainfall averages 40 to 50 inches, spread over most of the year. Precipitation is rarely heavy, but reaches a peak in fall and early winter.

A special hazard to sea and air navigation is provided by sudden squalls known as "williwaws," which sweep down from the mountainous area with great force, sometimes reaching gale proportions within half an hour. The mountains are concentrated on the north sides of the islands, and the williwaws cause strong off-shore winds which make it difficult to find a lee along the north coasts. The columns of spray and mist resulting from the williwaws frequently resemble huge waterfalls.

Winds generally are gusty because of the deflection of air currents by the steep mountain slopes. The greatest velocities occur in March. In the Aleutians, curiously enough, winds and fogs may persist together many days at a time. Humidity is always high. Temperatures are moderate and not subject to much variation. In this connection it should be remembered that, contrary to popular conception, the Aleutians are not arctic territory. In places they are only 02° north of the border between Canada and the United States proper. Kiska lies in the latitude of London and the longitude of New Zealand.

While Aleutian weather was a constant impediment to he military operations of the United States and Japan alike, the enemy enjoyed one advantage. Weather in this theater moves from west to east, with the result that the Japanese always knew in advance the conditions which were likely to prevail in the islands.

Chapter 1: The Attack on Dutch Harbor
June 1942

While the eventual goal of the Japanese activities in the Aleutians remains somewhat obscure, it is clear that the initial attack in June 1942 was subsidiary to the powerful thrust at Midway. The Central Pacific offensive was conducted by approximately 80 ships, including 4 or 5 carriers, at least 3 battleships, and a large number of cruisers, destroyers, auxiliaries, and transports. The simultaneous assault on the Aleutians employed a much smaller force, probably containing two small carriers, two seaplane tenders, several heavy and light cruisers, destroyers, and submarines belonging to the Fifth Fleet, and from four to six transports and cargo vessels. Obviously Midway was the primary objective.

The Midway attack was thrown back with great loss in what may prove to have been one of the decisive battles of the war. In the Aleutians area, however, the weakness of our forces, plus the ever-present handicaps of climate and geography, precluded our maintaining an airtight defense. In spite of heroic efforts, especially those of Army and Navy pilots, it is doubtful whether we prevented the enemy from attaining any of his immediate objectives, modified as they undoubtedly were by the Battle of Midway.

Preparations

CINCPAC on 21 May 1942 established Task Force Tare under the command of Rear Admiral Robert A. Theobald. Admiral Theobald was given control of all Army, Navy, and Canadian forces in the Alaskan-Aleutian theater and was ordered to prepare to defend the area against Japanese attack. The inadequacy of the strength available for this task is well demonstrated by a comparison with the naval and air forces present in the Philippines in December 1941, since the results of our weakness in that theater are well know. In the Philippines were stationed 73 naval vessels, including 3 cruisers, 13 destroyers, and 29 submarines, as well as 280 aircraft of all types. Task Force Tare, on the other hand, contained only 52 vessels and 169 planes. Its sole advantage was in cruisers, of which there were 5, 2 heavies and 3 lights. The rest of the naval force was composed of 11 destroyers, 6 submarines, 2 destroyer seaplane tenders, 1 gunboat, 1 minesweeper, 2 oilers, 10 Coast Guard vessels, and 14 district patrol craft. Planes, mostly Army types, consisted of 94 fighters, 7 four-motored bombers, 42 two-motored bombers, 23 patrol bombers (PBYs of PatWing Four), and 3 scouts.

Admiral Theobald's force not only was pitifully small but it had to be spread dangerously thin. Nevertheless, our situation at that time was such that no significant reinforcements could be assigned, although the area to be protected constituted one of the most important approaches to the United States.

The main surface vessels of Task Force Tare proceeded from Pearl Harbor to Kokiak. There, on 27 May 1942, Admiral Theobald issued an operation plan for the several groups under his command, since intelligence had by this time made it clear that a Japanese attack could be expected during the first few days of June, probably on the Umnak-Dutch Harbor-Cold Bay area.

Since Task Force Tare contained no carrier, Admiral Theobald was dependent on land or harbor-based planes for searches. His 23 PBYs were located principally at Dutch Harbor and Kokiak and were capable of reconnaissance over a radius of 400 miles. The Army possessed one base farther west, at Fort Glenn on Umnak Island, which had been constructed in such deep secrecy that it was believed to be unknown to the enemy. Twelve P-40s were stationed there. These planes were of slight value for search but were to prove helpful in attacking Japanese surface forces.

By 1 June the entire coast from Nome to Seattle was in a condition of 24-hour alert, with aircraft searching to the limit of their fuel endurance and other planes being hastily ferried in from the south. Great reliance was of necessity placed on radar installations in patrol planes, not only to prevent collisions with fog-shrouded mountains, but to make the searches themselves in any way effective, since the scarcity of aircraft and the poor visibility did not permit close visual search. Later events proved that this reliance was fully justified. Until the enemy occupation force was discovered at Kiska, every contact was made first by radar and later developed visually.

Dutch Harbor Bombed, 3 and 4 June

On 2 June two enemy carriers were reported less than 400 miles south of Kiska. All available 11th Air Force planes were immediately ordered to the advanced airfields at Cold Bay and Fort Glenn.

Aided by the first clear weather in three days, the Japanese attacked Dutch Harbor and nearby Fort Mears on the morning of 3 June almost simultaneously with their attack on Midway. In the harbor were the two old destroyers *King* and *Talbot*, the destroyer-seaplane tender *Gillis*, the submarine *S-27*, the Coast Guard cutter *Onondaga*, and the U.S. Army transports *President*

Fillmore and *Morlen*. When unidentified planes were detected at 0540 by the radar of the *Gillis* (Lt. Comdr. Norman F. Garton), she and the other ships weighed anchor and stood out with all hands at battle stations.

Ashore, the Naval Air Station had gone to General Quarters at 0430 in accordance with daily routine. At 0545, while battle stations were still fully manned, a flight of about 15 carrier-type fighter planes appeared. Any doubt as to their enemy character disappeared when they began to strafe our installations, and our batteries opened an intense antiaircraft fire. After a single flight over the station, during which they did very little damage, the planes moved off to the northward.

Japanese bombing of Dutch Harbor, 4 June 1942

At about 0550 four bombers approached on a course of 030°. Five minutes later they released 16 bombs. Two dropped into the water, but 14 fell in the congested area of Fort Mears, the white frame buildings of which made a conspicuous target. Two barracks and three Quonset huts were destroyed and several buildings were damaged by the hits and resulting fire. Approximately 25 men were killed and about the same number wounded. A second flight of three bombers overshot Fort Mears and did no material damage, but a third flight of three planes damaged the radio station and demolished a Quonset hut.

Burning buildings at Ft. Mears after first enemy attack on Dutch Harbor, 3 June

The last flight of planes apparently had as its target the wooden oil tanks, which had been there for years, so that the enemy could easily have known their location. The bombs overshot the tanks, but killed a man in a Navy fire watcher's pillbox and the driver of an Army truck. All told, about 15 fighters and 13 horizontal bombers participated in the raid. All the bombers were tracked in at about 9,000 feet. No fighters from Fort Glenn, 65 miles away, managed to intercept.

The ships (except the *Morlen* and *S-27*) had joined the shore batteries in firing at the planes. The Commander of the Naval Air Station remarked that "the *President Fillmore's* fire was notable. In addition to her own armament, she had mounted on deck a battery of 37-mm. guns consigned to Cold Bay, which gave her 22 antiaircraft guns. These were served with such rapidity that the *Fillmore* appeared to be (and was reported) on fire." The *Gillis* claimed two planes shot down. No ship was damaged.

The morning of 4 June was rainy and overcast. In spite of the reduced visibility, our Catalinas kept contact with the enemy force most of the morning, until a tracking plane was damaged by antiaircraft fire. During the day the weather improved, and by evening it was clear, with scattered clouds at 3,000 feet.

Damage to Ft. Mears caused by Japanese raid of 3 June

At 1740 Fisherman's Point Army Observation Post reported three flights of bombers headed for Dutch Harbor. Shortly before 1800 they were reported near Mt. Ballyhoo. At 1800 fire was opened as ten fighters attacked the Naval Air Station in a low strafing attack. Then 11 bombers delivered a dive-bombing attack through openings in the overcast. Each carried one large bomb, which was released after a shallow dive to 1,000 or 1,500 feet. The chief damage was to our four new 6,666-barrel fuel oil tanks, which had been filled for the firs time on 1 June by the *Brazos.* These, with their contents of 22,000 barrels of fuel, were totally destroyed. The adjacent Diesel oil tank was punctured and burned out, but bunkers fortunately prevented burning oil from reaching the remainder of the tank farm. An old station ship, the *Northwestern,* which had been beached for use as a barracks for contractors' personnel, was set afire and partly destroyed. The Japanese also scored hits on a warehouse and an empty aircraft hangar.

At 1821 three horizontal bombers approached from the northeast. Their five bombs fell harmlessly into the harbor. The final attack of the day came at 1825, when five planes, approaching at high altitude from the northwest, dropped bombs near the magazine area near the south slope of Mt. Ballyhoo. Nine bombs were ineffective, but the tenth killed an officer and three men in a Navy 20-mm. gun emplacement. Personnel casualties during all the attacks were 33 Army, 8 Navy, 1 Marine Corps, and 1 civilian killed, plus about 50 wounded.

Coincident with the second Dutch Harbor raid, Japanese fighters strafed shore installations at Fort Glenn on Umnak. Army pursuit planes took to the air and shot down two enemy aircraft. The remaining seven withdrew without inflicting damage. Because of the fog and the retirement of the hostile carriers, many enemy planes probably ended in the sea. As their gas ran low, frantic radio calls were heard.

The three Japanese attacks on 3 and 4 June constituted the enemy's sole offensive action in the central and eastern Aleutians in the entire period of the campaign. As has been suggested, the outcome of the Battle of Midway may have caused a change in the plans of the Japanese High Command. The discovery by the enemy of the air base on Umnak, 600 miles west of Kodiak and 100 miles west of Dutch Harbor, may also have exercised a restraining influence.

Meanwhile Admiral Theobald's main surface force, consisting of two heavy cruisers, three light cruisers, and four destroyers, was operating in the Gulf of Alaska about 400 miles southeast of Kodiak Island. This position was maintained in order to be able to intercept any hostile attempts to land troops on the mainland or otherwise challenge our shore defenses. Such sightings of enemy ships as occurred during this period were too far west for an attack by Task Force Tare, even if Admiral Theobald had chosen to meet the Japanese without the support of carrier aircraft. On both 3 and 4 June, our search planes, operating for the most part in extremely bad weather, reported sighting individual Japanese carriers or carrier groups about 200 miles southwest of Umnak. Brig. Gen. William O. Butler, Commander of the Air Striking Group of Task Force Tare, ordered his planes to attack these ships, but because of inaccurate contact reports and persistently unfavorable weather our bombers failed to inflict significant damage. Concerned by the course of events, Admiral Theobald decided to confer personally with his task group commanders at Kodiak, since enforced radio silence prevented contact with subordinates while at sea. He therefore departed from the main surface force in the *Nashville,* leaving Capt. Edward W. Hanson of the flagship *Indianapolis* in command. He started back from Kodiak the next afternoon (the 5th), after emphasizing the absolute necessity of maintaining the maximum number of planes in the areas where the enemy appeared to be operating.

Despite reports of occasional successes by Army bombers, operational and combat losses incurred in keeping contact had become increasingly serious. On 4 June Admiral Theobald intercepted a dispatch stating that only 14 PBYs remained operative. Pilots and crews were said to be at the limit of endurance after 48 hours of continuous operations in bad weather, while there had been numerous costly encounters between patrol planes and Zeros.

Although it is possible, in view of the low visibility, that the Army B-26s inflicted more damage than was apparent at the time, and that their counterattacks from Umnak surprised the enemy and were a factor in the retirement of his carriers, the situation had deteriorated to such an extent by 7 June that CINCPAC was requested to dispatch a carrier and additional cruisers to reinforce Task Force Tare. COMINCH suggested using the *Saratoga*. Stripping the West Coast of all patrol squadrons was authorized. The Army sent eight A-29s and four B-17s from Edmonton to Alaska, and six B-24s were ordered north from California. Later developments, however, rendered the naval reinforcements unnecessary.

Chapter 2: Enemy Occupation of Attu and Kiska

On 10 June the situation began to clarify, at least temporarily. A study of the reports strongly indicated that a powerful Japanese force, including one or two carriers, had operated south of Umnak and Unalaska on 3 and 4 June, and that U.S. Army bombers had damaged two probable cruisers during that time. A diminishing number of contacts thereafter suggested the enemy's withdrawal to the west. Apparent confirmation of this movement came on the 10th, when a search plane reported sighting several unidentified ships in Kiska Harbor. No weather reports from Attu and Kiska, where small meteorological outposts were maintained, had been received since the 7th.

On the 11th it became evident that the enemy had landed substantial forces on these two islands. A search plane reported one heavy cruiser, two light cruisers, one destroyer, and six transports in Kiska Harbor. (Actually the force consisted of 20 vessels, including the light cruisers *Kiso* and *Tama* of the Fifth Fleet, three destroyers, three corvettes, three minesweepers, and four cargo vessels.) A Navy plane sighted and bombed a light cruiser and a destroyer west of Kiska and observed an enemy landing force on Attu. Our submarines were immediately ordered to take maximum offensive action against the Japanese in the western Aleutians.

On 11 June the Catalinas of PatWing Four began a continuous 48-hour shuttle bombing of Kiska. The tender *Gillis* had arrived at Atka the previous day, and early in the morning she commenced refueling and rearming the PBYs as they arrived from the main base at Dutch Harbor. Soon a steady procession of patrol planes was flying between Atka and Kiska. At the end of the run they dived on enemy ships and beach parties at 250 knots, "dropping bombs by the seaman's eye method." After returning to Atka, the aircraft refueled and rearmed at once and took off as soon as possible. The strain upon pilots and crews was terrific, one pilot flying 19 ½ hours during a single 24-hour period.

This method of operation continued until the *Gillis* ran out of bombs and fuel. By the second night the flight crews were so exhausted that the tender's hands gave up their bunks so that the aviation personnel could get some rest.

Before retiring from Atka, the *Gillis* carried out a "scorched earth" policy, setting fire to all buildings. Little of value was left for the enemy if he should attempt to move eastward from Kiska. The aerological station on Kanaga Island also was evacuated.

By 12 June the Japanese had firmly established themselves on Kiska and Attu. On that date Army heavy bombers of the 11th Air Force made their first run over Kiska, claiming hits on two cruisers and one destroyer. One Liberator was lost to the intense antiaircraft fire which was sent up chiefly by the ships in the harbor. As a result of the flak and the continually bad visibility in the area, it was difficult to determine the results of our bombing. In this initial phase, Kiska was too far away for our Army heavies to subject it to sustained bombardment. Consequently almost the entire task devolved upon the PBYs, many of which had just arrived from California stations, so that the crews were wholly unfamiliar with the terrain. In view of later experience, it is unlikely that raids by these aircraft, although conducted with the utmost skill and bravery, possessed much more than nuisance value. Certainly none of the enemy's operations was impeded to a significant extent.

Japanese transport burning after U.S. air attack on Kiska Harbor, 18 June 1942

Despite frequent reconnaissance and bombing flights as far west as Attu, the situation had again become obscure and distinctly disturbing. On 14 June the Japanese bombed Nazan Bay, Atka. On 19 June it was reported that the hostile forces operating in the Aleutians consisted of three carriers, two battleships, five heavy cruisers, three light cruisers, twenty-two destroyers, and either seven or eleven submarines. It later appeared that these totals were considerably exaggerated; but there was no means of knowing this at the time, and we were far from being able to match the reputed enemy fleet. The report of Japanese strength provoked the comment by high authority that "the presence of this formidable force in Alaskan waters is a matter of grave concern and indicates definitely that the whole chain of the Aleutians is in danger of Japanese occupation." It was hardly encouraging to learn that the enemy was reconnoitering Adak, or that on 22 June hostile submarines had shelled Esteban, B.C., and an American destroyer lying in the mouth of the Columbia River in Oregon.

By the 30th of the month, however, it became apparent that if the Japanese had been operating a major striking force in the western Aleutians, it had returned to bases in the Empire. Patrol planes reported that while the enemy continued to consolidate his positions on Kiska and Attu, burning brush and preparing the ground for airfields, he was being supported only by a small force of light vessels. No heavy ships were located anywhere in the area.

Chapter 3: "Strong Attrition" — Kiska Bombarded

With the exception of the Battle of the Komandorskis, 26 March 1943, and the assault on Attu in May 1943, operations during the Aleutians Campaign consisted in the main of seizure of unoccupied islands by both sides, and bombardment and bombing of enemy-held islands by our forces. By commencing the first-mentioned process with the occupation of Kiska and Attu, the Japanese has stolen a march on us. It was some time before we were able to answer with counter-occupation of other bases. Meanwhile, in the words of Admiral Theobald, the duty of Task Force Tare was to take advantage of every favorable opportunity to inflict "strong attrition" on the enemy. This involved continuous, if light, bombing of Japanese positions and, eventually, the first of the long series of naval bombardments to which Kiska and Attu were subjected while in Japanese hands. It also placed upon our small force of submarines a great responsibility which they soon proved themselves fully capable of bearing. On 4 July the *Growler* (Lt. Comdr. Howard W. Gilmore) sank two Japanese destroyers and possibly a third off Kiska. On the same day the *Triton* (Lt.

Comdr. Charles C. Kirkpatrick), while on patrol near the island of Agattu, sent another destroyer to the bottom.

It was of the utmost importance to prevent the development of either Kiska or Attu as a major enemy base for further advances eastward. As Admiral Theobald well knew, a critical period would arrive when the Japanese realized that our main naval strength was being shifted from Pearl Harbor to the South Pacific for the coming Solomons Campaign. If the enemy should then decide to thrust toward the mainland from Kiska, forces available at Pearl Harbor would be insufficient to cut in on his flank. Land-based air power in the Alaskan-Aleutian theater was too weak to hold or indeed delay such an advance, and even if large naval forces had been available in the area, there were no facilities for their upkeep.

Results of the bombing of Kiska by Army and Navy planes proved so inconclusive that it was early decided to try the effect of gunfire by surface forces — the cruisers and destroyers of Task Force Tare.

The original date of the bombardment was 22 July. Bad weather forced successive postponements, first to 27 July, and finally to 7 August, when meteorological conditions were at last reported favorable. In the interim the bombardment force retired and refueled.

As of 1 August, the complete organization of Task Force Tare was as follows:

Task Force Tare, Rear Admiral Robert A. Theobald.

(a) *Air Group,* Brig. Gen. William O. Butler, USA.

(1) Air Striking Unit:

Bombardment: 28th Composite Group, 30th Bombardment Group (11 heavy bombers, 23 medium bombers).
Reconnaissance: 406th Bombardment Squadron; 8th Bomber Reconnaissance Squadron of the Royal Canadian Air Force (21 medium bombers).
Fighters: 11th, 18th, 42nd, 54th, 57th Fighter Squadrons; 111th

Fighter Squadron of the Royal Canadian Air Force (98 fighters).

(2) Air Search Unit, Capt. Leslie E. Gehres:

Patrol Squadrons 41, 43, 51, 62
(11 PBY flying boats, 20 PBY-5A amphibious flying boats).

Tenders:

Avocet, Lt. Comdr. William C. Jonson, Jr.
Casco, Comdr. Thomas S. Combs.
Gillis, Lt. Comdr. Norman F. Garton.
Hulbert, Lt. Comdr. James M. Lane.
Teal, Lt. Comdr. Albert S. Major, Jr.

Escort:

Kane, Lt. Comdr. John J. Greytak.

(b) *Escort and Patrol Group,* Rear Admiral John W. Reeves, Jr.

1 gunboat:

Charleston, Comdr. Gordon B. Sherwood.

1 minesweeper:

Oriole, Mellish M. Lindsay, Jr.

5 over-age destroyers:

Dent, Lt. Comdr. Paul H. Tobelman.
Gilmer, Lt. Comdr. Herman O. Parish.
Humphreys, Lt. Comdr. John K. Wells.
Sands, Lt. Comdr. John T. Bowers, Jr.
Talbot, Lt. Comdr. Edward A. McFall

Coast Guard vessels.
Patrol vessels

(c) *Submarine Group,* Comdr. Oswald S. Colclough.

5 submarines:

Finback, Comdr. Jesse L. Hull.

Grunion, Lt. Comdr. Mannert L. Abele.
Trigger, Lt. Comdr. Jack H. Lewis.
Triton, Lt. Comdr. Charles C. Kirkpatrick.
Tuna, Lt. Comdr. John L. DeTar.

(d) *Main Body*, Rear Admiral William W. Smith.

2 heavy cruisers:

Indianapolis (F), Capt. Morton L. Deyo.
Louisville, Capt. Elliott B. Nixon.

3 light cruisers:

Honolulu, Capt. Harold Dodd (Relieved 3 August 1942 by Capt. Robert W. Hayler).
Nashville, Capt. Francis S. Craven.
St. Louis, Capt. George A. Rood.

4 destroyers:

Case (F, Comdr. Wyatt Craig, ComDesDiv 6), Comdr. Robert W. Bedilion.
Gridley (F, Comdr. Frederick Moosbrugger, ComDesDiv 11), Lt. Comdr. Fred R. Stickney.
McCall, Lt. Comdr. William S. Veeder.
Reid, Comdr. Harold F. Pullen.

1 fast minesweeper:

Elliot, Lt. Comdr. Daniel J. Wagner.

(e) Tanker Group.

1 oiler:

Ramapo, Comdr. Harold A. Carlisle.

2 over-age destroyers:

Brooks, Lt. Comdr. Charles T. Singleton, Jr.
King, Lt. Comdr. Kenneth M. Gentry.

As background for the operations of Task Force Tare, the map sets forth the character and location on 1 August of Army and Navy bases in the Alaskan area.

Potential enemy strength in the Aleutians which might be faced by Task Force Tare in its attack on Kiska was estimated on 1 August to consist of one or two heavy cruisers (*Nachi* class), one light cruiser, eight destroyers (*Shigure* class), eight submarines, one seaplane tender, two cargo vessels, six submarine chasers (plus numerous other patrol vessels), four patrol planes, six single-float observation planes, and eight single-float fighter planes. It was considered possible that one or more auxiliary carriers also might be in Attu-Kiska waters. Other hazards to be faced included mines and coast defense guns of calibers probably not exceeding six inches.

The plan of action called for three coordinated bombardments of the shipping in Kiska Harbor and adjacent shore establishments. The four destroyers (*Case, Gridley, McCall, Reid*) were to approach to ranges of 14,800 to 14,500 yards. The light cruisers (*Honolulu, St. Louis, Nashville*) were to engage at a range of approximately 16,800 yards, while the heavy cruisers (*Indianapolis, Louisville*) were to commence firing at 19,500 to 18,900 yards.

The task group, with Admiral Smith as OTC, sortied from Kodiak during the afternoon and evening of 3 August and proceeded to the approach area, which it reached at 0800 on the 7th, weather conditions having moderated to an extent which enabled Admiral Smith to commit himself to immediate execution of the plan. H-hour was set for 1800 (Zone plus 10).

The Air Striking Unit had been directed to attack shipping and installations in the Kiska area, continuing the assault as late as possible in order to engage enemy forces to the maximum up to the time of the arrival of the bombardment group. Thereafter it was to cover the retirement of our surface forces, following up with renewed attacks on Kiska Harbor and vicinity.

Air search units were to operate from an advanced base established on Atka and provide full weather information on the target area. During retirement they were to maintain protective scouting 200 miles to the rear and 100 miles on the flanks of the bombardment group. On D plus 1 day they were to execute protective sweeps ahead of the surface forces. Meanwhile our submarines also were to make weather reports and maintain a close watch for enemy surface vessels.

The Approach

Weather conditions at noon on 7 August were as follows: wind from the northwest, force one to three; sea smooth; surface visibility 8 to 10 miles; sky completely overcast, ceiling about 500 feet. The overcast had persisted during the preceding two days, so that all positions were plotted by dead reckoning.

At 1630 Admiral Smith's group reached latitude 51°10' N., longitude 177°19' E. and proceeded north at a speed of 20 knots, as visibility steadily deteriorated. At 1750, 10 spotting planes were launched. No landfall was made. However, radar ranges and bearings were taken on what was believed to be Kiska Mountain and Segula Peak.

After a few minutes Admiral Smith turned south, since visibility was zero and it was inadvisable to continue at great navigational risk and bombard from a dead reckoning position. Surface visibility around Kiska had been reported by a patrol plane to be only one mile. Accompanying patrol planes were then forced by low fuel to return to base.

At 1825 Lieut. Robert A. O'Neill, leader of the *Indianapolis* spotting flight, reported that Kiska Harbor was visible through breaks in the overcast. Ten transports or cargo vessels, four submarines, and a large destroyer or light cruiser were seen in the harbor, with one destroyer and one smaller ship patrolling off the entrance. This was the first report in four days on the character and number of enemy ships present. Lieut. O'Neill also stated that there were no signs of bombing by the Air Striking Unit.

By this time our cruiser planes had been fired on by antiaircraft and attacked by float planes. Because the presence of SOC type aircraft must have warned the enemy of the proximity of surface forces, Admiral Smith decided to attempt a second approach. Just before he turned north, the fog cleared, producing visibility of about five miles to the north and east. Cruiser planes also reported visibility of 10-15 miles east of Vega Point. At 1934 the destroyers emerged from the fog, which had closed down again 14 minutes before, and obtained a fix on Kiska Island. They were now close to the firing position.

At 1942 the force executed a simultaneous turn to course east, the first leg of the firing plan. Five minutes later the heavy cruisers also ran clear of the fog.

The Bombardment

At 1955 the destroyers opened fire, followed two minutes later by the three light cruisers, and at 2000 by the *Indianapolis* and *Louisville*. Although the ceiling over Kiska Harbor was low, and fog patches were present, numerous antiaircraft bursts were soon observed, indicating that the island's defenders believed that a high-level bombing attack was going on.

Spotting either from ships or cruiser planes proved most difficult because of visibility conditions. The experience of the *Louisville*, as reported by her commanding officer, well illustrates the handicaps under which the bombardment was delivered, as well as the impossibility of accurately checking the results achieved:

Mental impressions formed through careful and repeated study of charts of Kiska Harbor and Island were of little value. As ship pierced fog bank just before opening fire, land was revealed all along the port hand. No member of the fire control party was able to recognize any topographical feature until some minutes later. Twin Rocks were reported by lookouts as "enemy cruisers standing out," and later as "enemy cruiser turned over." As the accuracy of fire will never be ascertained, proper analysis of performance cannot be determined.

The bombardment lasted for about half an hour, during which 631 rounds of 8-inch, 3,534 of 6-inch, and 2,620 of 5-inch were expended. By 2036 all cruiser planes had been recovered, except one *Indianapolis* aircraft. The force then began its retirement. Army Air Force planes, which had been prevented by fog from reaching their bombing objectives, returned to Kiska three days after the bombardment and obtained a series of photos, which, although obscured by clouds, were considered evidence of fairly extensive damage. To summarize:

1 destroyer hit, possibly sunk.
1 transport hit and probably destroyed (beached and deck awash).
1 transport possibly sunk.
Various batteries silenced.
Moderate damage to shore installations, with unknown damage to stores and equipment.

There was no way of knowing whether this damage resulted entirely from the bombardment itself or was partly caused by previous Army air attacks.

The St. Louis fires a salvo at Kiska during the bombardment of 7 August 1942

On 10 October the Army finally succeeded in taking a series of entirely satisfactory photos. As interpreted, these pictures showed a total of approximately 1,600 shell holes, most of which were located in an area centered about 2,600 feet northeast of the edge of the Japanese camp area. Thus a large portion of the bombardment was over its objectives. No shell holes were noted in the vicinity of shore installations, but such evidence would not necessarily have been allowed to remain for so long a period in an area in constant use.

The results of the shelling were so inconclusive as to evoke from Admiral Smith comments of this nature:

"(1) The bombardment of Kiska by a surface force of heavy ships would be of questionable value unless followed by the landing of troops. Results to be expected from indirect bombardment would not balance the risk to heavy ships under difficult conditions of approach in mineable waters, where enemy destroyers might be encountered in low visibility.

"(2) Light cruisers were considered more adaptable to conditions in the area than heavy cruisers. With the prevalent low visibility, ships which could quickly produce a great volume of fire would have a decided advantage.

"(3) The enemy could not be driven out of Kiska by surface bombardment alone. Visibility conditions permitting, more damage to shore installations could probably be inflicted by a squadron of bombers.

"(4) Attacks from the north by motor torpedo boats supported by destroyers could make Kiska Harbor untenable for the enemy."

CINCPAC commented as follows: "Coming simultaneously with our movement into the Solomons, this action to the north, in addition to the damage caused, probably had some diversionary effect, as there appeared to be considerable delay in the movement of the majority of the Japanese carriers and other heavy units to the South Pacific."

Chapter 4: Occupation of Adak
30 August 1942

On 5 August the Joint Chiefs of Staff had approved a plan to occupy Tanaga Island and construct an airfield there in order to deny the area to the enemy and to provide advance base support for offensive operations by our forces. This plan was to be carried out at such time as Task Force Tare could be augmented, "after certain commitments elsewhere had been met." Preparations, however, were to begin immediately. Extensive searches revealed no enemy operations east of Kiska, although it was probable that the Japanese had scouted other islands. Meanwhile, our submarines continued their aggressive support of the policy of "strong attrition."

On 15 August the *Gato* (Lt. Comdr. William G. Myers) sank the 9,300-ton *Kinka Maru* in latitude 51°05′ N., longitude 162°07′ E. The next day the *Triton,* patrolling 60 miles northwest of Kiska, torpedoed an enemy cruiser or destroyer, which was said to have "disintegrated."

On 21 August, Admiral Theobald issued an operation plan covering the projected move to the west, which was now to culminate in the occupation of Adak. D-day was to be 30 August. It was assumed that the Japanese might have lookouts as far east as Adak itself and that they might be planning the early construction of airfields on that island and on Amchitka. On 28 August soldiers from the Alaska Defense Command, together with 40 combat intelligence scouts, landed at Kuluk Bay. No signs of the enemy were discovered. Search planes reported that Amchitka also was ostensibly unoccupied.

Army makes unopposed landing on Adak, 30 August 1942

Available for the operation at Adak was approximately the same strength at the beginning of the month. A few more planes were now on hand, however, as well as the destroyer *Lawrence* (Lt. Comdr. Henry T. Jarrell), one additional submarine, two more minesweepers, the Canadian auxiliary cruisers *Prince David*, *Prince Henry*, and *Prince Robert*, and two Canadian corvettes. The transports *J. Franklin Bell* (Capt. Herbert J. Grassie), *St. Mihiel* (Comdr. Edward B. Rogers), and *Thomas Jefferson* (Comdr. Chauncey R. Crutcher), the Army transport *North Coast*, and the merchant vessels *Branch* and *Stanley Griffith* had also arrived to carry the occupation force, which was to be commanded by Brig. Gen. Eugene Landrum, USA. The escort force, under Capt. Francis S. Craven of the *Nashville*, was to consist of that ship, the *St. Louis*, and the *Brooks, Dent* (now commanded by Lt. Comdr. Thurlow W. Davison), and *Kane.* The covering group, commanded by Rear Admiral Smith, was composed of the *Indianapolis, Louisville, Honolulu, Gridley, McCall,* and *Reid* (now commanded by Lt. Comdr. Harry H. McIlhenny). The transport group, under Capt. Herbert J. Grassie, was to include, in addition to the ships mentioned above, the over-age destroyers *Humphreys* (now commanded by Lt. Comdr. Robert C. Peden), *King, Lawrence,* and *Sands.*

The Air Striking Group had effected a concentration of all available heavy bombers and P-38s at Umnak in preparation for possible enemy opposition. As it turned out, the landing proper was accomplished without incident, but on the first day the tender *Casco* (Comdr. Willis E. Cleaves) was struck by a small submarine torpedo while in Nazan Bay, Atka, and had to be beached. She was not refloated until 13 September.

The Casco beached on Atka during Adak landing, 30 August 1942

As soon as the troops were ashore, work was begun on the first Adak airfield. By almost superhuman effort, the runway was completed by 12 September, thus advancing our westernmost base to within 250 miles of Kiska and altering the whole complexion of the air war.

Chapter 5: From Adak to Amchitka
September 1942-January 1943

Our forces were still operating under the "strong attrition" directive and continued to do so until the spring of 1943. But the seizure of Adak accelerated the rate of attrition appreciably. As soon as the airbase was operative, the Army began a new and considerably heavier bombing campaign against Kiska. The first raid of major proportions took place on 14 September. Three cargo vessels were hit, two minesweepers apparently sunk, and three midget submarines strafed.

The Japanese had not been idle, however. During August they had reinforced Kiska with 1,000 Marines and 500 civilian laborers. The island was redesignated the 51st Naval Base and placed under the command of Rear Admiral Akiyama. It was clear that our base at Adak had been occupied just in time if we were to counter the enemy's obvious intent to accelerate the completion of air facilities in the western islands.

In mid-September the enemy moved the 301st Independent Infantry Battalion from Attu to Kiska, temporarily abandoning the former island. On the 25th of that month a strong force of

Army and RCAF bombers and fighters hit the newly strengthened garrison, destroying eight seaplanes, strafing two submarines, and setting serious fires on one of two transports found in the harbor.

It was not until 2 October that it became definitely established that the Japanese knew of our occupation of Adak, though the heavier raids by our bombers must have given them food for thought. On that date the first of a number of enemy nuisance bombings occurred. We retaliated with minor raids almost daily. On the 10th six separate attacks were launched. Six days later, a particularly strong formation sank an enemy cargo vessel and a destroyer and damaged another destroyer. The 11th Air Force continued to whittle away at the enemy's air strength also, whenever opportunity provided. At no time were the Japanese permitted to operate more than 14 planes. Usually they were so weak in the air that their pilots avoided combat.

The precarious situation of our forces in the South Pacific now began to exercise a serious influence on the Aleutians Campaign. In mid-October it was suggested that a bombardment of Kiska by two or three old battleships would help make the island untenable by the enemy. This plan was turned down for a variety of reasons, most of which were related to critical conditions in the south. Since our principal naval concentration was in that area, it was felt that all available old battleships should be retained at Pearl Harbor to guard against the remote likelihood of a Japanese attack. Also no 16-inch HC ammunition was on hand, and only small quantities of 14-inch. Furthermore, the somewhat optimistic impression prevailed that our air attacks were already making Kiska too hot for the Japanese.

Thus the policy of "strong attrition" could not at this time be bolstered by a big-gun bombardment. An even more serious blow to North Pacific operations was the necessary detachment of several vessels for service in the Solomons. On 12 October the *Louisville* (now commanded by Capt. Charles T. Joy) headed south. On the 24th the *St. Louis* followed, as did the tender

Thornton (Comdr. Wendell F. Kline), which was needed because of damage to the *McFarland* (Lt. Comdr. John C. Alderman). This left only the tender *Gillis* (now commanded by Lt. Comdr. Herman L. Ray) in operative condition in the Aleutians. The *Indianapolis* and *Nashville* (now commanded by Capt. Herman A. Spanagel) were also scheduled to leave as soon as they could be replaced by the *Raleigh* and *Detroit*.

The tenseness of the South Pacific situation was further highlighted by the departure of 12 F4F-4 replacements gleaned from the Alaskan theater's none too adequate air force.

On 30 October five Canadian ships, including the three auxiliary cruisers, were released. The *Nashville* and *Indianapolis* were detached on 17 November (the latter ship only temporarily), and the *Raleigh* (Capt. Ward P. Davis) reported on that date.

Since our surface forces had been so depleted, our attrition tactics during November were carried on from the air alone. Our planes were unable to drive the Japanese off Kiska and Attu, which had again been occupied by the enemy; but they and our submarines were thoroughly successful in preventing the enemy from building up his offensive potentialities, which our base at Adak and a new airfield on Tanaga Island, even closer to Kiska, continued to be rapidly developed. Finally, on 17 November, events had reached a state where Admiral Theobald could be directed to prepare a plan for the occupation of Kiska, to be preceded by the seizure of Amchitka.

As December opened, however, our naval striking force in the Aleutians consisted only of the *Detroit* (Capt. Ellis H. Geiselman), *Raleigh* (Capt. Ward P. Davis), *Bailey* (Lt. Comdr. John C. Atkeson), *Bancroft* (Comdr. John L. Melgaard), *Caldwell* (Lt. Comdr. John E. Newman, Jr.), and *Coghlan* (Lt. Comdr. Benjamin F. Tompkins), a group too weak for offense and indeed hardly powerful enough to oppose any serious Japanese attack on our position on Adak. And in the first days of the month it appeared that such an attack was imminent, or at least that an effort would be made to occupy the Semichi Islands. On the 4th of the month a search plane located what appeared to be a large enemy convoy in latitude 49° N., longitude 180′, about 160 miles southeast of Amchitka. The commanding general, 11th Air Force, was ordered to hit this force with every available plane, but before the attack was launched, the report was discovered to be erroneous. Further alarms and excursions enlivened the next few days without discovery of any actual hostile move.

On 9 December Rear Admiral Charles H. McMorris replaced Rear Admiral Smith as commander of Task Force Tare's striking group, which will hereafter be referred to as Task Group Mike. On the 17th Amchitka Island was surveyed by U.S. reconnaissance parties. Evidence of Japanese visits within the past month was plain. Test holes had been dug on several sites suitable for airfields. No advance posts or coastwatchers were unearthed, however. Since the situation appeared favorable, Admiral Theobald was directed on the 23d to occupy Amchitka as soon as forces could be assembled.

During the period of preparation, the fast minesweeper *Wasmuth* (Lt. Comdr. Joseph W. Leverton, Jr.) was lost. On 27 December she was proceeding at six knots in very heavy weather when several depth charges fell overboard and exploded, snapping the keel. The ship broke up and sank. Fortunately all personnel were saved.

Chapter 6: Occupation of Amchitka
12 January 1943

The transport group for the occupation of Amchitka was commanded by Capt. Paul K. Perry, USCG, while Army forces were under Brig. Gen. Jones. Transport and cargo vessels were the *Arthur Middleton* (Capt. Perry), the Army transport *Delarof*, the merchant ship *Lakona*, and the cargo vessel *Vega* (Comdr. Arthur C. Smith), while protection was provided by the destroyers *Dewey* (Lt. Comdr. Joseph P. Canty), *Gillespie* (Comdr. Chester L. Clement), and *Kalk* (Comdr. Charles T. Singleton, Jr.). Rear Admiral John W. Reeves, Jr., commanded the Alaskan Sector Escort Group of one gunboat, one minesweeper, and three fast minesweepers, while Rear Admiral McMorris commanded the Striking Group, *Indianapolis* (now commanded by Capt. Nicholas Vytlacil), *Raleigh*, *Detroit*, and four destroyers. On 4 January, Rear Admiral Thomas C. Kinkaid relieved Rear Admiral Theobald in supreme command.

On the 12th troops were landed in Constantine Harbor from the *Arthur Middleton* without opposition, but the transport later went aground, undergoing some damage and considerable delay in unloading. She was not refloated until the end of the month.

Unopposed landing at Constantine Harbor, Amchitka, 12 January 1943

The enemy's only reaction to the occupation of Amchitka was a series of minor air attacks, which began on 24 January with his discovery of our occupation, and continued into February. Meanwhile our growing air power hammered Kiska and Japanese shipping whenever the severe winter weather would permit. Considerable attention was devoted to the incomplete fighter strips which aerial photos had discovered on Kiska and Attu on 19 January.

On 17 February Warhawks and Lightnings landed on our new Amchitka fighter strip, constructed under the most arduous conditions. Thereupon the enemy's light bombings ceased. The occupation of Amchitka, like that of Adak, permitted acceleration of our bombing campaign and improved our reconnaissance. Within two months thereafter, the enemy's supply problems had been rendered practically insoluble.

Chapter 7: First Bombardment of Attu
18 February 1943

In early February it was realized that since the enemy now knew of our occupation of Amchitka he could be expected to take counter measures. One of the most likely steps appeared to be an increase in Japanese forces and installations on Attu, notably in the Holtz Bay and Chichagof Harbor areas. Therefore it was decided that Task Group Mike (Rear Admiral McMorris) should weaken these positions by direct naval bombardment. The task group was now organized as follows:

Task Group Mike

One heavy cruiser:

Indianapolis, Capt. Nicholas Vytlacil.

One light cruiser:

Richmond (F), Capt. Theodore M. Waldschmidt.

Four destroyers:

Bancroft, Comdr. John L. Melgaard.
Caldwell, Comdr. John F. Newman, Jr.

Coghlan, Comdr. Benjamin F. Tompkins.
Gillespie, Comdr. Chester L. Clement.

D-day was tentatively designated as 21 February and H-hour as 15 minutes before sunrise, if visibility and other factors permitted. The Holtz Bay area was to be the first target, followed by Chichagof Harbor. Any ships present were automatically to become the primary targets of our cruisers.

On 13 February the task group proceeded in accordance with an earlier operation plan which directed it to steam west of Attu to intercept and destroy enemy *Marus* believed to be supplying Japanese positions on the islands. Contacts were negative, except with aircraft. Since the latter had undoubtedly reported Task Group Mike's presence in the area, our force returned on 18 February to conduct the bombardment of Attu, where enemy shipping had been reported by the submarine *S-128* (Lieut. John D. Crowley). The shelling was conducted without opposition in the air, on the sea, or from shore batteries, although desultory antiaircraft fire was directed against spotting planes.

The approach was made from the west, and later in the day than had originally been planned. Cruisers were in column with the *Richmond* as guide. The destroyers were disposed around the cruisers as antiaircraft screen. The formation was later modified to place two destroyers in the van and the other two astern of the cruisers.

Task Group Mike first steamed past the objective to ascertain if enemy shipping was present in either Holtz Bay or Chichagof Harbor. No contacts were made. At 1431 a Liberator flew over the center of the formation without identifying itself and was fired on before recognition was possible. Fortunately no hits were scored. At 1452 the ships reversed course by simultaneous movement for the firing run. The wind was about 12 knots from the northeast. The sea was smooth, and visibility excellent. Under the revised plan, Chichagof Harbor was the first target. Firing began at 1504 and continued for ten minutes at ranges varying from 10,000 to 12,000 yards. At 1625 Holtz Bay was taken under fire and shelled for 11 minutes at a range of 9,000-11,500 yards.

During the bombardment, the *Indianapolis* used a proportion of AP shells in order to distinguish her salvos from those of the *Richmond*. A few projectiles landed on the beach, throwing up red clouds of snow which facilitated identification by spotting planes and Top Spot. No prominent targets were visible, however, and no conclusive results were observed.

Two *Indianapolis* spotting planes dropped two 100-pound bombs on buildings in the Chichagof region. They also strafed some landing boats, but without apparent damage.

Chapter 8: Destruction of Enemy Ammunition Ship
19 February 1943

After concluding the bombardment, Task Group Mike continued its eastward retirement from its patrol area. When night fell, course was reversed and patrol west of Attu was resumed. The group was now divided into two sections, with the *Richmond, Bancroft,* and *Caldwell* operating to the south of the *Indianapolis, Coghlan,* and *Gillespie.* Capt. Vytlacil of the *Indianapolis,* commanding the northern unit, ordered extreme vigilance, since he anticipated that the maneuvers of the group might have deceived the Japanese into thinking that Task Group Mike had cleared the area and that it was safe for supply vessels to run the gauntlet to the western islands.

At 2000 on 19 February the *Indianapolis* was in latitude 51°23′ N., longitude 171°09′ E., about 120 miles southwest of Attu. Scouting course was 000° T., with speed 16. The *Gillespie* was screening the *Indianapolis,* while the *Coghlan* steamed six miles to the southward. At 2037 the *Gillespie* was ordered to a position six miles north. About an hour later the *Indianapolis* changed course to 162° T.

In the vicinity of the *Coghlan* the weather was excellent, with a full moon contributing high visibility. A moderate sea was running. At 2220 the *Coghlan* made SC radar contact on two objects, 9.6 miles away. An immediate report was flashed to the *Indianapolis* by TBS. The contact later developed as a single vessel. Capt. Vytlacil ordered the destroyers to concentrate on him.

At 2223 the *Indianapolis* went to General Quarters. Two minutes later a smoke smudge was sighted on the starboard bow. Simultaneously the cruiser's SG radar picked up an object bearing 204° T., range 25,900 yards. The *Indianapolis* closed rapidly on course 220° T., later changed to 210°.

In 20 minutes the *Coghlan* had taken a position ahead and the *Gillespie* astern. Various changes of course and speed followed in response to evasive maneuvers begun by the strange ship at 2259. By 2312 the *Indianapolis* had closed sufficiently to challenge the vessel, which proved to be about 400 feet long and of 3,000-5,000 tons. The answer, consisting of Japanese code for Able, was unsatisfactory. Consequently, at 2316, the American ships opened fire. The *Indianapolis* scored a direct hit with the third main battery salvo, and the enemy vessel began to burn. Our destroyers were also finding the mark with their 5-inch 38s, as was the *Indianapolis* secondary battery.

The Japanese ship fired three or four rounds from a small gun on its bow, plus a long burst from an automatic weapon. All shots fell far short. By 2325 the target had stopped. A minute later the *Indianapolis* fired a salvo which struck a vital spot. The enemy vessel began to blaze furiously from stem to stern to the accompaniment of continuous minor explosions, indicating that the cargo included fuel and ammunition. Our task group ceased fire (the *Indianapolis* had expended 37 rounds of 8-inch HC and 70 of 8-inch AP), but the enemy ship did not appear to be sinking. Her fires illuminated the entire area, and there was danger that our ships would be subject to submarine attack if they remained in the area much longer. It was therefore decided to sink the hulk with torpedoes.

The results of this endeavor were disappointing. At 2359 the *Coghlan* fired one torpedo at a range of 3,000 yards, depth 10 feet, speed 46. The run was hot, straight, and normal, but the torpedo passed under the target without exploding. Eleven minutes later another was launched with a depth setting of five feet. It detonated 500 yards short, possibly as a result of striking wreckage. A third torpedo set at two feet was fired from 2,000 yards to explode on contact. It passed about 10 yards astern.

The *Gillespie* then launched a torpedo which appeared to head for the target but missed. A second torpedo began porpoising and zigzagging and passed astern.

Finally, the *Coghlan* was ordered to sink the wreck with gunfire. Four 4-gun salvos aimed at the water line produced several hits. Fires and explosions resulted, but the hulk remained afloat.

The *Coghlan* then tried again with a torpedo set at zero depth. This detonated 50 yards short with some probable damaging effect. At 0124 the destroyer fired two more 5-inch salvos, and the enemy vessel finally sank by the stern. The *Coghlan* proceeded to search for survivors, but found none. A life jacket, marked lumber, and one bamboo life raft were recovered by grapnel. The life jacket was Japanese army equipment.

Our ships reformed their scouting line and continued their patrol.

Chapter 9: The Battle of the Komandorskis
26 March 1943

Introduction

As March began, the effects of harassing attacks on the enemy's lines of communication by our combined air, surface, and undersea forces made it likely that the Japanese would soon make a more serious attempt to bring reinforcements to their beleaguered garrisons. To forestall such a move, Task Group Mike was to initiate further patrols west of Attu.

Reorganization of the group began early in the month, when the destroyer *Bailey,* which had just been overhauled, joined the *Richmond* and the *Coghlan* at Dutch Harbor, where the latter two vessels had also undergone extensive overhaul. On 14 March these three ships held day/night target practice, after which they proceeded to patrol areas southwestward of Kiska, stopping en route at Adak on 16 March to refuel. Antiaircraft and torpedo drills were held during the patrol.

The enemy became aware of our presence in these waters on 21 March when a Japanese float plane tracked the three ships in the vicinity of latitude 51° N., longitude 176° E.

The *Salt Lake City*, Dale, and Monaghan joined on the 22d to complete the makeup of Task Group Mike, which was now organized as follows:

1 heavy cruiser:

Salt Lake City, Capt. Bertram J. Rodgers.

1 light cruiser:

Richmond (FF), Capt. Theodore M. Waldschmidt.

4 destroyers, Capt. Ralph S. Riggs (ComDesRon 14):

Bailey (F), Lt. Comdr. John C. Atkeson.
Coghlan, Comdr. Benjamin F. Tomplins.
Dale, Comdr. Anthony L. Rorschach.
Monaghan, Lt. Comdr. Peter H. Horn.

The Salt Lake City

Half the *Salt Lake City's* crew, including seventy percent of her fire control personnel, was at sea for the first time. The new men had come aboard at Pearl Harbor, where the cruiser had had a four-month period of repair and overhaul necessitated by damage sustained in the Battle of Cape Esperance. After putting to sea on 11 March, the *Salt Lake City* spent one week at intensive target practice in the Hawaiian area and then proceeded without escort to Dutch Harbor.

Events Preceeding the Action

On 22 March, with his force complete, Admiral McMorris set course to the west. This was in accordance with Admiral Kinkaid's operation plan, which required that the group should proceed to the west of Attu and intercept any enemy ships which might approach the Japanese bases in the Aleutians.

From analysis of the meager information available regarding the previous routes and methods used by the Japanese, and from personal observations made on previous patrols in that area, the task group commander chose the northwesterly approaches to Kiska and Attu. The patrol was to extend at least as far west as 168° E. Consideration of radar capabilities, navigational difficulties, and the possible necessity for rapid concentration, led to the choice of six miles as the distance between ships on the scouting line.

On the 25th the *Salt Lake City* refuled the *Bailey* and *Coghlan*. this operation had been in prospect for several days, but rough weather had intervened. In the midst of fueling, the task group commander received orders from Commander Task Force King, directing Task Group Mike to return to port.

Admiral McMorris acknowledged, but decided to delay execution of the order until fueling was completed. This proved to be an important decision, since Admiral Kinkaid, before the destroyers had been topped off, sent another message authorizing continuation of the patrol. In view of subsequent events, the fueling operation and the determination to continue the patrol were most fortunate.

Task Group Mike assumed a scouting line with the intention of searching the area as thoroughly as the number of ships and amount of fuel available would permit. A tentative schedule for the group called for refueling of the *Monaghan* and *Dale* by the *Salt Lake City* on the 28th. It was also anticipated that the

Richmond would have to withdraw from the patrol and return to Adak for fuel late on the 29th. Two destroyers were to escort her. In this case, the *Salt Lake City* and the two remaining destroyers would continue the patrol several days longer, until the other three ships returned to station, if possible.

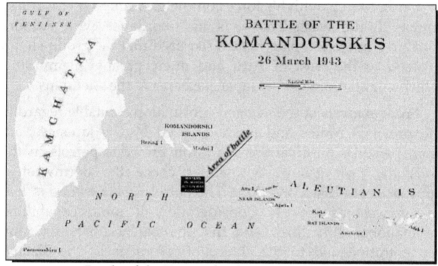

Battle of the Komandorskis, 26 March 1943

Preliminary Movements of the Battle

At 0600 on 26 March, Task Group Mike assumed base course 020° T. Ships were in scouting line on axis 35-°-170° T., distance between units being the customary six miles. Their order from the north was: *Coghlan, Richmond, Bailey, Dale, Salt Lake City*, and *Monaghan*. All ships were making 15 knots and zigzagging according to plan. A 7-8 knot wind was blowing from the southeast over a sea which was calm except for gentle swells from the northeast. Surface visibility was excellent although a heavy overcast hung at 4,000-5,000 feet.

At 0730, exactly one hour before sunrise, the *Coghlan*, northernmost ship in line, established SC radar contact with two ships, bearing 010° T., range 14,500 yards. She immediately sent word via TBS to Admiral McMorris in the *Richmond*. The flagship, still the second ship in line from the north and the guide of the group, was in position 53°16' N., 168°32' E. at that time.

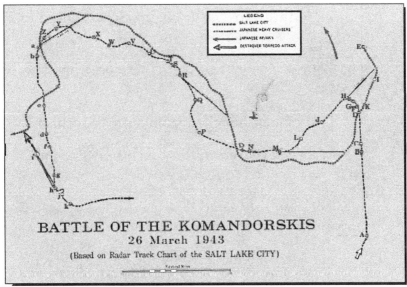

Battle of the Komandorskis, 26 March 1943
Based on Radar Track Chart of the Salt Lake City

	LETTERS REFER TO CIRCLED LETTERS ON CHART
A	Task Group Mike turned to base course 000° T. Half-hour to sunrise.
B	*Richmond* had 9 vessels (unidentified as to type) in sight.
C	At approximately this time two heavy cruisers were discerned in the enemy force.
D	Task Group Mike changed course to 330° T., to intercept Japanese AP/AK's.
E	Enemy CA's opened fire on *Richmond*, range approximately 20,000 yards. Flagship replied immediately.

F		Japanese CA's shifted fire to the *Salt Lake City*. Our heavy replied and hit an enemy CA with at least two 8-inch shells on the third or fourth salvo.
G		40° left turn to 290° T. begun. Speed raised to 25 knots.
H		Course changed to 250° T. Speed upped to 28 knots.
I		Two planes launched from Japanese cruisers.
J		*Richmond* ceased fire as range to nearest enemy ship had opened to 22,800 yards.
K		*Salt Lake City* straddled enemy CA repeatedly. Japanese ship began smoking badly.
L		*Salt Lake City* hit at frame 102 on the port side.
M		Course changed to 280° T. Many straddles on the *Salt Lake City*.
N		Course changed to 300° T. Speed had increased to 33 knots.
O		Spotting plane about 12,000 yards to starboard was hit by AA fired by *Salt Lake City*, *Bailey*, and *Coghlan*. The scout disappeared smoking.
P		Course changed to 320° T. to close exposed Japanese light cruiser.
Q		Course changed to 020° T. Speed now 28 knots.
R		*Salt Lake City* suffers a steering casualty. Ship headed hard right.
S		*Salt Lake City* hit by shell which penetrated her main deck forward.

T	ComDesRon 14 assumed tactical command of the *Bailey* and *Coghlan* and those two ships stood by to lay smoke screen for the *Salt Lake City*.
U	*Salt Lake City, Bailey,* and *Coghlan* commenced making smoke. Our heavy cruiser entered it at 1020.
V	Course changed to 240° T. so that the *Salt Lake City* could take advantage of the smoke as it then lay.
W	ComDesRon 14 assumed tactical command of all four destroyers. *Monoghan* and *Dale* were immediately ordered to lay smoke, which they began to do shortly.
X	*Bailey, Richmond, Coghlan,* and *Dale,* in that order, became engaged with an enemy light cruiser.
Y	*Salt Lake City* hit by another 8-inch shell, this time on the starboard catapult. Aircraft and catapult damaged. Plane caught fire and was jettisoned.
Z	Course changed to 210° T. as task group commander decided to head south. Speed changed to 30 knots.
a	*Salt Lake City* hit at port frame 102 again, but this shell did not penetrate the hull. Indirect damage extensive.
b	Course changed to 180° T.
c	*Salt Lake City's* after engine room out of operation because of battle damage. Her speed dropped to 20 knots.

d	*Coghlan* and *Bailey* started in for a torpedo attack on the enemy heavies.
e	Enemy CAs turned right to avoid the threatened attack.
f	Torpedo attack belayed as the *Salt Lake City* picked up speed. Our destroyers again joined formation astern.
g	At approximately this time, the *Salt Lake City's* engines stopped.
h	*Salt Lake City* swung left for a last-ditch defense just before she came to a dead stop in the water. HC projectiles fired by the after batteries because of a shortage of AP shells caused the enemy to fire AA, as he apparently thought he was being bombed by planes. Task group commander ordered ComDesRon 14 to carry out a torpedo attack on the enemy. The *Bailey*, *Coghlan*, and *Monaghan*, in that order, started in for the assault. The *Dale* was left to screen the *Salt Lake City*.
i	The *Bailey*, hit badly, fired five torpedoes and turned back toward our cruisers. The *Coghlan* and *Monaghan* did not expend torpedoes because of the unfavorable circumstances but also came left for retirement. The *Bailey* was hit by more shell fragments as she turned. The *Coghlan* also was damaged topside.
j	*Salt Lake City*, now making 15 knots, fired her last salvo of the battle. *Richmond* standing by to screen her and the retiring destroyers, if necessary.
k	Action ended. Task Group Mike retires eastward on base course 090° T.

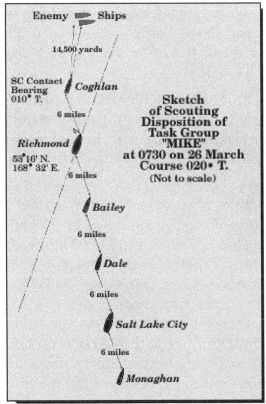

Enemy 🚢 Ships

14,500 yards

SC Contact
Bearing
010° T. ⎢ Coghlan

6 miles

Richmond

53°16' N.
168° 32' E.

6 miles

⎢ Bailey

6 miles

⎢ Dale

6 miles

⎢ Salt Lake City

6 miles

⎢ Monaghan

**Sketch
of Scouting
Disposition of
Task Group
"MIKE"
at 0730 on 26 March
Course 020° T.**
(Not to scale)

*Sketch of Scouting Disposition of Task Group Mike
at 0730 on 26 March; Course 020° T.*

A few seconds after her radar contact, the *Coghlan* picked up the vessels visually. And beyond these ships, two or three others could be seen, hull down on the horizon. None could be identified as to type. The *Richmond,* meanwhile, had also established contact by means of her SG radar. Three pips were on the screen, bearing 359° T., distant 24,000 yards.

One minute after the initial contact, at 0731, Admiral McMorris ordered all ships to go to Boiler Condition One and concentrate on the *Richmond.* Lookouts on the flagship discerned the dim outlines of five ships at 0732, but darkness prevented identification.

Most of our ships were already at General Quarters. Regular morning routine had sent the crew of the *Dale* to their posts at

0720, while the *Richmond, Monaghan,* and *Bailey* were in process of manning their dawn battle stations at 0730. By 0733 the remaining two ships, the *Salt Lake City* and *Coghlan,* had also gone to General Quarters.

For a short time after this first flurry of activity, all the other ships in the group were busy with course changes to close the flagship. The *Monaghan,* the last in line, was 24 miles south of the *Richmond.* All ships in the group were striving to build up their speed.

After 10 minutes of tracking by the *Richmond's* radar, contact course was estimated to be 080° T., speed 13 knots. During this period, the flagship had closed to 21,000 yards. There were five pips on her screen at that time. Upon receipt of this information, Admiral McMorris ordered Task Group Mike's course changed to parallel that of the unidentified ships. At 0745, when the *Bailey* and *Coghlan* were within a few thousand yards of the *Richmond,* the Admiral urged the *Monaghan, Dale,* and *Salt Lake City* to expedite concentration as much as possible. To comply, these ships increased speed and adopted more sharply converging courses.

About 0750, shortly after our course change to 080° T., the enemy force turned left and headed north. It was difficult at this time to get a clear conception of the enemy's composition, as maneuvers within his group hampered our lookouts and resulted in confusion on our radar screens. His change in course and the reshuffling of his forces made it clear, however, that he had sighted our vessels.

This alteration of course by the enemy resulted in the range opening rapidly, until by 0800 our flagship and the nearest Japanese ship were 27,000 yards apart. To counteract this, Admiral McMorris ordered a base course of 000° T. Although this change further delayed concentration, it was necessary if contact was to be maintained. The *Richmond's* speed was held to 15 knots to allow the lagging ships to close formation astern. While these variations in course were taking place, the *Salt Lake City, Monaghan,* and *Dale* had built their speeds up to 29, 27, and

22 knots respectively. The *Coghlan* and *Bailey* were maneuvering to take station on the flagship, the estimated position of which was 53°20' N., 168°36' E.

At 0803 Admiral McMorris radioed Admiral Kinkaid, stating merely that Task Group Mike had made contact with an enemy force and was concentrating to attack it. Nothing at the time indicated that the opposition was formidable. Although the haze of morning twilight was fading fast, the mist which had not as yet been dissipated and smudges of smoke among the enemy vessels, evidently from cold boilers being forced, combined to handicap vision. Observers on the *Richmond* had agreed on one point only—that auxiliaries were present in the Japanese group. Their reports on the enemy's over-all composition, however, were conflicting. None mentioned any warship larger than a light cruiser.

By 0805 the *Bailey* was in the van 3,000 yards ahead of the flagship and 500 yards ahead of the *Coghlan*. One minute later, her lookouts sighted two vessels, either APs or AKs, on course 355° T., distant 26,000 yards. The *Bailey* went to 20 knots.

In the meantime, our ships astern were making steady progress in closing formation. The *Salt Lake City* had gone to 30.5 knots at 0805; the *Monaghan* was making 29 knots at the same time and rapidly building up speed. The *Dale*, some distance behind the *Richmond* but still ahead of our heavy cruiser, was steaming at approximately 22 knots.

As our leading ships shortened the gap between them and the enemy, the *Richmond's* SG radar began to show additional pips. Men on the flagship's signal watch reported at 0811 that the opposing force was composed of one single stack destroyer and four merchantmen. One of the supposed APs or AKs was large and the other three were small. Five minutes later, after slowing to 15 knots, the *Bailey* made visual contact with five ships. Nine Japanese vessels were in sight from the *Richmond* by 0820.

Concern was now felt lest an enemy ship escape, and the Japanese auxiliaries were designated as primary objectives. As Admiral McMorris put it, "The task group commander still felt that a Roman holiday was in prospect."

Wishing to strike quickly, Admiral McMorris acted to facilitate the concentration of his group. Accordingly, the *Dale* and *Monaghan* were directed to remain astern of the fast-closing *Salt Lake City*, which was still several miles behind the flagship. In executing this order, the *Dale* slowed to 15 knots and circled left to drop astern of the *Salt Lake City*. The *Monaghan* was already steaming several miles behind the heavy cruiser.

The first indication of the actual strength of the enemy came a few minutes after 0820, when lookouts on the *Richmond* identified first one, then two, of the opposing ships as heavy cruisers. Other still unidentified fighting ships could be seen around the two cruisers. "The situation had now clarified, but had also radically and unpleasantly changed," commented Admiral McMorris.

The Japanese force now held the advantages of better tactical position, greater numerical strength, and overwhelmingly superior firepower. Directly ahead of our group were the enemy combatant ships on a southeasterly course which was closing the range rapidly. Meanwhile, the merchantmen were steaming north-northwest, about 25,000-30,000 yards distant from the *Richmond*. Two destroyers, which had previously been screening the merchant vessels, doubled back and joined the foe's combatant group, leaving the merchant vessels unescorted. This move by the Japanese light units caused some confusion among our ships when they reported the strength of the enemy.

At 0825, about the time that the task group commander was discovering the presence of heavy ships among the enemy, the *Richmond* had a torpedo alert. Lookouts reported a periscope off the port quarter, and Capt. Waldschmidt immediately rang up 20 knots. One minute later, however, the flagship's speed was again set at 15 knots when the report proved false.

As the ships in the rear of our column closed, they began to catch glimpses of the foe. The *Monaghan* and *Dale* sighted the enemy's smoke and masts simultaneously at 0826. By 0830 the *Bailey* had six ships besides the auxiliaries in sight. One of the six challenged our group with a searchlight. This overture was ignored, as were subsequent signals of the same type. The *Coghlan,* following in the *Bailey's* wake, was in contact with eight ships at this time. Radar range to the nearest of the eight was 23,900 yards. To the *Salt Lake City,* now fairly close astern of the *Richmond,* the Japanese appeared to be two or three AKs and one destroyer. She began making out various other enemy warships within the space of two or three minutes, however.

In the short space of time since first sighting the enemy heavy cruisers, three courses of action had suggested themselves to Admiral McMorris. Task Group Mike could fight, withdraw, or attempt to maintain long-range contact. In making a decision, he had to consider another discouraging aspect of the situation: at best it would be at least two or three hours before our aircraft based on Adak could be expected to arrive.

Despite the unfavorable factors, Admiral McMorris decided to make an attempt to attack the enemy auxiliaries. There were numerous reasons for this course. It was possible that judicious maneuvers by our group might bring the merchantmen within gun range before the Japanese combatant ships could intervene. Forcing the enemy's hand, moreover, might lead him to dispatch some of his fighting ships to convoy the auxiliaries in their retirement. Such a move on his part would provide Task Group Mike an opportunity to fight the remainder on more nearly even terms. Furthermore, a feint by our ships to the west might cause the Japanese to send their auxiliaries on to Holtz Bay, where they would have been subject to submarines and air attacks.

To close the objectives, a change of course to 330° T. was signaled at 0833. However, the fact that the *Salt Lake City* was still some distance astern precluded an increase in speed, which would have been desirable. By 0839 Task Group Mike was squared away on its new course, concentration virtually complete. Our ships were now disposed with the two cruisers in column approximately 1,000 yards apart, the *Richmond* leading. The van destroyers, the *Bailey* and *Coghlan,* were on station off the port bow of the flagship, while the two rear destroyers steamed off the starboard quarter of the *Salt Lake City.*

To some of our ships the enemy's composition and disposition were still obscure. His combatant vessels were headed southeastward, a course opposite to that of our group, and steaming in a loose formation at about 15 knots. His heavy cruisers, which were in the lead, were followed closely by one light cruiser. The other light cruiser and the destroyers brought up the rear and were on the disengaged side of the heavy cruisers. It appeared that the Japanese light forces were trying to concentrate on the heavy cruisers in order to take up battle formation.

Action is Joined

The opposing forces converged rapidly. At 0840 the Japanese heavy cruisers opened fire on the *Richmond* at a range of approximately 20,000 yards. The first salvo was on in deflection but 1,000 yards short. The excellence of the enemy's gunnery was soon attested, however, for the second salvo straddled the *Richmond.*

Our light cruiser replied immediately with her forward and after twins and the starboard singles, a total of seven 6-inch guns. She chose the leading heavy cruiser as her target. It was on bearing 045° R., distance 19,700 yards (by SG radar).

One minute after action started, at 0841, Commander Task Group ordered both the *Richmond* and the *Salt Lake City* to launch their aircraft. But Admiral McMorris countermanded this order to the *Richmond* before her planes took off, in the belief that the flagship's two scouts would be needed more urgently later in the battle. Circumstances prevented the *Salt Lake City* from launching any aircraft. Heavy weather encountered a few days before had damaged one of her catapults and one of her planes, putting both out of operation. Her second scout could not take off because it had been degassed.

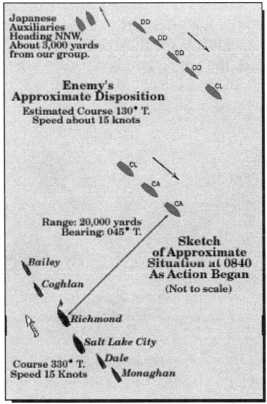

Enemy's Approximate Disposition

After obtaining the correct range on the *Richmond,* the enemy proceeded to lay several straddles across her in quick succession. Some of the shells landed close aboard and shook the ship considerably. On the bridge it was thought that she had taken hits on the bow and amidships. Capt. Waldschmidt. zigzagged his vessel to throw off the enemy's fire control, while damage control parties checked on the ship's injuries. A cut smokestack guy, probably severed by a shell which went between stacks Nos. 3 and 4, was the only casualty found.

Shortly after making these straddles on the flagship, the Japanese heavy cruisers shifted their fire to the *Salt Lake City,* the initial salvos falling short by 1,000-1,500 yards. At 0842 the forward turrets of our heavy cruiser took the leading Japanese heavy cruiser under fire on an SG radar range of 21,000 yards. A few moments later, the after turrets were also brought to bear. Results came quickly. On the third or fourth salvo at least two 8-inch shells struck the target. Fire broke out in the vicinity of the enemy cruiser's bridge, but the flames proved disappointingly short-lived.

Enemy salvo lands astern of the Salt Lake City during the Battle of the Komandorskis

In spite of this quick success, the general situation was unfavorable, and retirement seemed expedient. The superior firepower of the Japanese force and the decreasing ranges between the two opposing groups made it merely a question of time until our ships suffered serious damage. Pre-battle maneuvers which, on our part, had been designed to bring the supposedly lightly-guarded auxiliaries within gun range, had interposed the enemy combatant ships between our group and its bases to the east. Obviously withdrawal in that direction was impossible. Accordingly, at 0843, Commander Task Group ordered a speed of 25 knots and a left turn of 40 degrees. This move also served the immediate purpose of complicating Japanese fire control.

As our group swung to its new course of 290° T., the van destroyers entered the battle. Both the *Bailey* and *Coghlan* opened fire on enemy heavy cruisers, at ranges of 15,000 and 18,000 yards respectively. After some five minutes, the *Bailey* directed her fire at a light cruiser in line behind the two heavy cruisers. These two destroyers kept firing until about 0841, when all targets were out of their range.

Meantime, a signal had been given at 0848 to change course to 250° T. and speed to 28 knots. Our ships realigned while carrying out this order. The *Dale* and *Monaghan* took station off the port quarter of the *Salt Lake City*, while the *Coghlan* and *Bailey* dropped back and took up positions off the starboard quarter of the heavy cruiser. The *Richmond* was now our leading ship, approximately 1,000 yards ahead of the *Salt Lake City*. Subsequently, the Japanese ships also turned, first southwestward, then in a northwesterly direction, and followed our group.

Concurrently with our van destroyers' action and the group's course changes, the *Salt Lake City* had obtained eight straddles on the leading Japanese heavy cruiser. These were from the first 18 salvos, controlled by Director I. Control was shifted to Director II as the ships sheered left. Additional straddles were observed on the same target. Smoke billowed from near her forward stack. The *Richmond* also switched control to Director II as she turned. Both our cruisers were under heavy fire at this time.

At 0856, while the *Salt Lake City* was bearing the brunt of the enemy's fire and the *Dale* and *Monaghan* were avoiding the salvos aimed at our heavy cruiser, two enemy observation planes were launched from separate Japanese cruisers.

About 0858 observers on our flagship reported torpedoes passing under her bow. Capt. Waldschmidt saw these purported "torpedoes" and declared that they actually consisted of "the splash of a school of small fish swimming in a comparatively straight and narrow path."

Our ships had gradually increased their speed until by 0858 Task Group Mike was making 30 knots, on base course 240° T. Individual ships were "chasing the splashes" so effectively that none of them had taken a hit as yet. The radical course changes which the *Salt Lake City* employed so successfully had a disadvantage, however, for she tended to lag behind the *Richmond.*

Many salvos were now landing within a radius of 200-300 yards of the *Salt Lake City's* bow, so Capt. Rodgers ordered the gasoline stowage blanketed with CO_2. Two Japanese heavy cruisers were focusing their fire on our heavy cruiser, walking their salvos up and down in 200-300 yard steps. Occasionally a light cruiser would also edge in close enough to lob shells at her. Personnel below decks could feel the concussion through the hull as shells detonated in the water nearby. Capt. Rodgers rang up flank speed.

The *Salt Lake City* was engaged ceaselessly as our group moved westward ahead of the enemy. The foe was in the following formation, from north to south: one light cruiser, two heavy cruisers, and another light cruiser. The four destroyers were stationed to port of the southernmost cruiser, well out of gun range.

At 0903 the *Richmond* ceased fire. She had drawn ahead until the range to the nearest enemy ship was 22,800 yards. Enemy fire directed at the flagship had become spasmodic as she left the pursuers farther astern. Soon the Japanese cruiser shifted fire from the *Richmond* to the *Salt Lake City.*

Enemy float planes now became bothersome. After being catapulted from the cruisers, they had circled to port and climbed into spotting position. One of these aircraft took station at extreme range abeam of the *Monaghan,* and in a short time the enemy salvos began moving closer to the *Salt Lake City.* Many of the overs and shorts landed uncomfortably close to our screening destroyers. At 0905 the *Monaghan* opened fire on this spotter with her 5-inch 38's. The enemy pilot put his plan through violent evasive maneuvers and withdrew temporarily. The aircraft was apparently undamaged. The *Salt Lake City* sighted two observation planes at this time, while the *Dale* saw one. Both ships held their fire, however, because the spotters hovered just out of range.

One of the enemy heavy cruisers was straddled repeatedly at 0907 by 5-gun salvos from the *Salt Lake City's* after turrets, her only 8-inch guns which would bear. After the range was established, several shells from our ship struck this target amidships. Shortly thereafter, black smoke began issuing from the enemy cruiser.

Meanwhile one of the Japanese planes had worked itself around to the starboard side of the *Richmond*. The flagship took it under fire at 0908 with her 3-inch guns at an SC radar range of 11,000 yards. These guns ceased firing two minutes later, when the plane banked steeply away.

Skillful conning, plus a modicum of luck, had saved the *Salt Lake City* from damage thus far in the battle. But, at 0910, personnel on the bridge felt the impact of hits both fore and aft. In a few minutes repair parties reported that the ship had been holed below the water line on the port side at frame 102. The shell had penetrated inward, ruptured oil tanks and bulkheads, nicked the port shaft, and exploded about three feet abaft the athwartship engine room bulkhead. Fragments flew in every direction, piercing nearby bulkheads. Shaft alleys Nos., 3 and 4 began flooding. Oil from punctured fuel tanks abaft the after bulkhead sprayed into the after engine room. Water leaking from pipes which had been carried away added to the difficulty, and, with the oil, formed a slimy coating on the deck. No damage was found forward at this time, however. Apparently the shocks felt there had come from near hits.

Three minutes later, as Task Group Mike was executing a change in course to 260° T., the starboard 5-inch guns on our heavy cruiser opened on a plane at a range of 12,000 yards. Ten rounds were sufficient to drive the intruder out of range.

At 0920 our ships altered course to 280° T., as the task group commander again sought to open the range. The enemy heavy cruiser which had been hit heavily at 0908 was still smoking badly. It began to lose speed, and the other heavy cruiser slowed to remain in company.

The *Salt Lake City*, meanwhile, was receiving the undivided attention of the enemy heavy cruisers. Two of the tight-patterned enemy salvos straddled her at 0921, shaking the ship considerably. Again the after engine room reported being hit. However, it was later ascertained that this had been a near hit.

The *Dale*, closest flanking destroyer to port, had quite a few shells land close aboard as the enemy cruisers walked their ladders up and down methodically on the zigzagging *Salt Lake City*. Lt. Comdr. Horn, commanding the *Dale*, described the enemy shooting as "beautiful," and said that it was a "miracle" that our heavy cruiser was able to avoid the salvos so effectively. At 0922 a venturesome enemy pilot flew in to about 9,500 yards from the *Dale*, and that destroyer and the *Monaghan* opened fire. The plane retired forthwith to a more discreet distance.

The *Salt Lake City* was swinging to 300° T., the new base course of the group, when the damage in her after engine room was declared to be under control. This was at 0927. Wads of clothing thrust into the breach in the after bulkhead had reduced the flow of oil into the engine room to mere seepage. Our heavy cruiser was making maximum speed, while the remainder of the task group was also steaming at about 33 knots.

The enemy was still disposed in three ragged columns. Viewed from the *Dale*, one light cruiser bore 050° T., range 28,000 yards; the two heavy cruisers bore 060° T., range 24,000 yards; and the other light cruiser and the destroyers bore 067° T., range 30,000 yards.

Another brush with an aircraft developed at 031, when the *Salt Lake City's* 5-inch guns opened to starboard on a float-type plane at a range of 9,500 to 12,000 yards. Our two screening destroyers to starboard, the *Bailey* and *Coghlan*, also took this target under fire. These three ships fired for only approximately a minute and a half. Their small expenditure of ammunition left its mark, however, for the plane swerved away into the clouds, trailing a plume of smoke behind it. A few minutes later, observers on our heavy cruiser saw a large splash and a tell-tale column of black smoke on the horizon. Thereafter, the other spotter remained at a range of about 18,000 yards.

About this time the southernmost enemy light cruiser and the four trailing destroyers began closing the *Salt Lake City*. As these five ships drew nearer off the starboard quarter, the other Japanese units also began to close slowly. This situation did not obtain for long, however, since by 0941 the range had again opened to 20,500 yards. The enemy temporarily checked fire.

Meanwhile, Commander Task Group Mike had radioed a dispatch to Commander Task Force King at 0937, giving the group's course and position, and advising that it was engaged in a long-range battle. An encouraging answer stated that supporting bombers could be expected about 1430, while Catalinas might arrive before that time. Admiral Kinkaid's communication also recommended that retiring action be considered. This suggestion "brought a smile" to Admiral McMorris' face.

Our ships were now steaming with the *Coghlan* and *Bailey* 1,000 and 1,500 yards respectively off the *Salt Lake City's* starboard bow, while the *Dale* and *Monaghan* occupied the same relative positions off the starboard quarter. The *Richmond* steamed 1,000 yards ahead and slightly to port of the *Salt Lake City*. Speed was still better than 30 knots.

At 0943 Commander Task Group signaled an alteration in course to 320° T. This was done in an effort to close an exposed enemy light cruiser on the northern flank of the Japanese formation. That ship was in a position to give range spots. The

Salt Lake City was still firing with her after guns as she went into this turn to the right.

The new heading finally unmasked the *Salt Lake City's* forward guns, and at 0946 she opened on the light cruiser with both forward and after 8-inch turrets. Eight 10-gun broadsides were fired at an approximate range of 18,000 yards. Some of these salvos straddled the target, and at about 0950, our heavy cruiser reported to the task group commander that she had hit one of the Japanese heavy cruisers and that she was pulling away from that ship. Seizing the opportunity this opening of the range afforded, Admiral McMorris decided to try to turn the enemy's right flank by heading northward.

Accordingly, a base course of 340° T. was ordered at 0950. The *Salt Lake City*, the forward turrets of which had again gone into the blind, requested permission to make a further change of course so that she might bring all her guns to bear on the light cruiser. After the exchange of several messages, Admiral McMorris advised our heavy cruiser to make such maneuvers as were necessary in order to use her firepower to the best advantage. Successive swings to the right were made in the following few minutes until, by 0956, the base course became 020° T. Both the flagship and the *Salt Lake City* were making 28 knots at that time.

A few moments after 1000, the light cruiser on which the *Salt Lake City* was firing veered sharply right, away from our ship's shells, and went into a tight circle. However, our potentially favorable position quickly deteriorated. The enemy heavy cruiser, which had been emitting clouds of smoke, recovered speed despite her fires and, with the other heavy cruiser, began moving closer. The Japanese force was now aligned with the light cruiser which had described the 360-degree turn in the van. Approximately a thousand yards astern of that ship were the two heavy cruisers. To the rear of the heavy cruisers, the other light cruiser and the four destroyers closed warily, remaining out of gun range.

By 1000 both Japanese heavy cruisers were repeatedly straddling the *Salt Lake City*. At 1002, while the enemy was forging steadily nearer and the pattern of his shellfire was moving closer, the *Salt Lake City* suffered a steering casualty. Her own gun blasts had carried away the rudder stops, and the rudder no longer responded to the wheel. The ship commenced heading sharply right, away from the base course. Less than 20,000 yards separated her from the enemy heavy cruisers, when at 1003, rudder control was shifted to Steering Aft.

Admiral McMorris viewed the erratic movements of the *Salt Lake City* and the rapidly closing range with apprehension. At this time also, a few salvos landed close aboard the *Richmond*, one of them jarring the ship. A prompt opening of the range was imperative, so course was changed to 330° T. without delay.

Meanwhile, the *Salt Lake City* had regained partial control of her steering gear. Use of the rudder was limited to 10 degrees to either side, however, lest it jam hard over. As she came slowly left to the new course, our heavy cruiser was under the concentrated fire of both the enemy heavies. While in the turn, she managed to fire one 10-gun broadside before the target bearing became such that only her after guns could bear. This fact made the battle even more uneven, for the Japanese ships possessed superior speed and were able to fire full salvos in conformance with their zigzag course. The *Salt Lake City* and the destroyers grouped about her sustained many near hits. Capt. Rodgers conned his ship cannily, alternately "chasing the salvos" and zigzagging. This procedure was so effective that his ship took no hits at that time, even though "shells could be seen falling like rain" around her.

The *Salt Lake City* was returning to base course by 1006. One minute later, Admiral McMorris ordered her to fire on the leading Japanese light cruiser, the nearest enemy ship to our group. A further 30-degree course change to the left was signaled at 1009. All our ships swung to the new heading, although the *Salt Lake City* was still experiencing difficulty with her rudder.

At 1010 the *Salt Lake City* reported her steering troubles to Commander Task Group Mike. Immediately after this message was sent, a shell penetrated our heavy cruiser's main deck forward. The projectile, which struck at starboard frame 7, had fallen at a high angle. It glanced off the starboard anchor windlass and was deflected forward and downward, passing outward through the hull at frame 4. The hole was two or three feet below the water line, and resulted in the flooding of several compartments. Bulkheads nearby were shored up promptly. There was no fire.

"Stand By to Lay Smoke"

As the situation became more serious, Admiral McMorris acted to protect the *Salt Lake City*. At 1012 he directed ComDesRon 14 to take tactical command of the *Bailey* and *Coghlan,* and stand by to screen the damaged cruiser with smoke. In preparation for this project, the two destroyers dropped back along the starboard side of the formation. In concert with the move, the *Monaghan* and *Dale* came up astern of the flagship.

After cutting the speed of the task group to 25 knots to keep our ships concentrated, the task group commander directed that smoke be laid. This was at 1015. Within three minutes, the *Bailey* and *Coghlan* began execution of the order. The *Salt Lake City* had begun generating chemical smoke a few moments earlier. Thereafter, the two destroyers shuttled around the heavy cruiser, usually at high speeds, laying an effective cover with a combination of stack smoke and chemical smoke from the FS generators. At 1020, the *Salt Lake City,* still using emergency steering with a maximum rudder of 10 degrees to either side, nosed into the screen. Range from the *Richmond* to the enemy at this time was 22,800 yards.

When the *Salt Lake City* entered the smoke screen, the Japanese fire diminished, but did not cease. As the battle moved westward, the enemy heavy cruisers fired sporadically, whenever gaps in the smoke afforded them glimpses of the *Salt Lake City*. Supplementing these visual contacts were spots given by the enemy's remaining plane and his light cruisers. These last-mentioned ships maneuvered constantly in an attempt to outflank the smoke screen and thus give fire control data. From the expeditious and accurate manner in which the Japanese heavies shifted their fire during this phase, many observers in our group deduced that at least one of those ships possessed fire control radar.

While the enemy was engaged in this manner, the *Salt Lake City* was being conned to take every advantage of the destroyers' smoke. The screen was being laid in parallel banks, one to port by the *Coghlan,* and the other to starboard by the *Bailey.* Capt. Rodgers maneuvered his ship as adroitly as possible, within the limits of the smoke, in an endeavor to throw off the enemy's aim. Shells continued to land on all sides of the ships, however. Our cruiser's after batteries answered persistently through the smoke. At 1028 base course was changed to 240° T., in order to bring the *Salt Lake City* more completely within the screen as it then lay.

About this time the enemy light cruiser, followed by the four destroyers, swung off to the south at a tangent from the main Japanese group. To some of our ships this portended an outflanking attempt or, possibly, a torpedo attack. At 1034, the *Salt Lake City* requested that two destroyers be kept between her and the enemy. These ships were to act as a buffer for her and, if feasible, fend off the foe with a torpedo attack.

At 1035, to assure our heavy cruiser the best possible defense, the task group commander directed ComDesRon 14 to assume tactical command of all four destroyers. Capt. Riggs immediately ordered the *Monaghan* and *Dale* to join the *Bailey* and *Coghlan* and assist in laying smoke. Accordingly, the *Dale* and *Monaghan* slowed and commenced dropping back along the port side of the formation. Meanwhile, the *Bailey* had swung left at 36 knots across the stern of the *Salt Lake City.* Shortly thereafter she took station to port, on the heavy cruiser's engaged side. This move brought the enemy observation plane within range to port, and a few moments' fire sufficed to drive it off.

At 1037, as the *Bailey* was changing her position, course was again altered to 300° T. A minute later, the group increased its speed to 28 knots. It was hoped that these two measures would put more water between Task Group Mike and the enemy, whose course was estimated as 330° T. Soon, however, a hostile light cruiser was seen to round the end of the smoke screen and close range.

The *Bailey* engaged this vessel at 1040. The target was on bearing 0786° T., range about 14,000 yards. Admiral McMorris at once ordered the *Salt Lake City* to shift her fire to this light cruiser. This TBS message was never received, although our heavy cruiser's equipment had functioned properly just a few moments before, when she reported her battle damage to Commander Task Group. However, the *Richmond's* after guns opened on the enemy ship at 1044, range 16,000 yards, bearing 080° T. A minute later the *Coghlan* joined in with her No. 3 and No. 4 guns.

Meanwhile, at 1043, ComDesRon 14 had directed the *Dale* and *Monaghan* to take station off the port quarter of the *Salt Lake City* in order to improve the smoke screen. To avoid delay, the *Monaghan* went hard right, while the *Dale* circled in the opposite direction. As the *Monaghan* started her turn, a grinding sound was heard in her starboard reduction gear. The engineer officer slowed the starboard engine to investigate. When advised of this action, however, the Bridge ordered maximum speed resumed on the engine. The cause of the trouble was not discovered at that time, and the engine operated noisily for the rest of the battle.

By 1046 the heavily-engaged enemy light cruiser was straddling the *Bailey*. Our destroyer was not hit, but her gyro went out a few minutes later, probably from the shock of near hits. The *Bailey* zigzagged to evade the salvos. The *Dale*, which was now astern of the *Salt Lake City*, joined battle with the same light cruiser at 1050. Her after guns opened at 16,000 yards, but smoke obscured the results.

The *Monaghan,* also dropping astern as ordered, began laying smoke at 1051. Since she had not reached her designated position, however, this operation was suspended a minute later. At this time, 1952, the *Dale* adjudged herself to be situated correctly, and started to make smoke. The *Monaghan,* after more maneuvering, took station at 1055, approximately 800 yards off the port quarter of the *Salt Lake City.* She resumed laying smoke. The enemy had dropped back by this time, until the range from the *Dale* increased to 20,000 yards. The destroyer then ceased fire.

While the *Monaghan* and *Dale* were reforming, Task Group Mike had been swinging to a new heading of 240° T. Speed was maintained at 28 knots.

The enemy heavies continued their systematic fire. At 1059 an 8-inch shell hit and exploded on the *Salt Lake City's* starboard catapult. The plane on the catapult burst into flames. Fragments of the projectile were flung in every direction, penetrating the well deck, and tearing jagged holes in the port catapult. Some particles embedded themselves in the forward stack and superstructure. Damage control parties acted with dispatch, however, and extinguished the fire in less than 10 minutes. The shattered plane was jettisoned at 1101. One officer and one enlisted man were killed, and four enlisted men were wounded.

At the time of this incident, our ships were steaming with the *Richmond* in the van, the *Salt Lake City* several thousand yards astern of the flagship, and the four destroyers off the port beam and quarter of the heavy cruiser. As seen through the smoke, the Japanese force appeared to be continuing on a northwesterly course, at an approximate speed of 30 knots. The enemy's rear heavy cruiser bore 085° T. from our flagship.

Admiral McMorris perceived that the general northwesterly trend in the direction of battle held a growing threat to Task Group Mike. According to his estimate, the scene of action at that time (latitude 53°42′ N., longitude 167°40′ E.) was approximately 125 miles closer to Paramushiru than to Adak. It seemed reasonable to assume that the Japanese had also radioed for air support. If so, their bombers would in all likelihood arrive before ours. It was decided, therefore, to break away by turning southward and later, as circumstances permitted, eastward.

Accordingly, a 30-degree left turn to 210° T. was signaled at 1102. Speed was increased to 30 knots. These moves provided an additional if transitory advantage. Because our change of course was hidden by the smoke, the enemy continued on his northwesterly heading for a few minutes after our ships turned south. This circumstance opened the range somewhat, and the *Richmond* ceased sustained fire. Between 1044 and 1102, fire control aboard the flagship had been shifted back and forth between Director I and Director II as necessity dictated. During that period the vessel expended approximately 80 rounds of 6-inch ammunition on the Japanese light cruiser which had rounded the smoke screen, obtaining at least three straddles. From 1102 on, the *Richmond's* after guns fired intermittently on both heavy and light cruisers, whenever suitable targets presented themselves. Smoke obscured the results.

As the *Salt Lake City* swung to the new heading at 1103, another shell struck her on the port side aft. The projectile did not rupture the hull, but glanced off and exploded alongside the ships. Plates at frame 98 were dented to a depth of nine inches. Indirect damage caused by this hit was extensive. The impact of the shell on the hull lent impetus to the flooding which had resulted from the previous hit at frame 102. Shortly after the second projectile struck, oil began spurting into the after gyro room. All electrical circuits to the after gyros and antiaircraft switchboard were opened as a precautionary measure.

At 1106 the antiaircraft switchboard compartment was abandoned. Attempts were made to shore up the after bulkhead of the engine room, but these proved awkward and inadequate because of the many pipe lines and manifolds in the vicinity.

Engine room pumps could not cope with the situation, so a submersible pump was hurriedly brought from a repair station. The rapid rise of the oil and water inundated the antiaircraft switchboard room, the after 5-inch handling room, the after 5-inch ammunition stowage, and shaft alleys No. 3 and No. 4. The ship took a four or five degree list to port.

At the time, this trouble aft did not adversely affect the *Salt Lake City's* speed or further impair her already limited maneuverability. By 1107 she was squared away on course 210° T., making the required 30 knots. A minute later, at 1108, the task group commander ordered another left turn made, this one of 30 degrees. As this flag hoist was being run up, the *Bailey* ceased fire on the light cruiser with which she had been engaged. Her gyro, which had been inoperative since 1050, began functioning again.

At 1110 an enemy light cruiser opened on the *Dale,* which, with the other three destroyers, was still making smoke off the port quarter of the *Salt Lake City.* The enemy's initial salvo, loaded with yellow dye, fell about 100 yards short off the port quarter. Our destroyer answered immediately at a range of 17,400 yards, on bearing 010° T. Guns No. 3 and No. 4 did most of the work, firing in unison, at six-second intervals. After the first enemy salvo, the Japanese cruiser walked her fire pattern up and down in steps of approximately 200 yards. Some of the enemy's shells landed over, about 100 yards off the starboard beam of the *Dale.* The destroyer employed abrupt turns and chased the salvos so well that no projectile struck her. The *Dale* and her adversary were engaged until 1121, when smoke hid them from each other.

In the meantime, the *Salt Lake City,* which had had a brief respite, swerved off course at 1116, when several salvos from an enemy heavy cruiser landed close aboard. Two minutes later, however, when the *Salt Lake City's* guns were replying, her heading was again 180° T.

At 1121, shortly after hour heavy cruiser got back on course, signal was made for Task Group Mike to turn 20 degrees left to

160° T. Admiral McMorris dispatched another of a series of messages to the task force commander at this time, informing him as to position, course, and pertinent particulars of the battle.

The enemy was now headed in a general southeasterly direction, again closing range. In the ensuing few minutes, it appeared that one of the Japanese light cruisers and three destroyers attempted to get into position to launch torpedoes. Observers in our group kept a vigilant watch on these ships, but the attack did not materialize.

No sooner had this danger abated, however, than a greater cause for alarm arose within the group itself. At 1125 the *Salt Lake City's* after engine room went out of operation. Water, and cold, glutinous oil had flooded the compartment to a depth of five feet—just below the level of the main engines. It was necessary to stop the after engines in an effort to remedy this condition. Speed dropped to 20 knots. At the same time, oil was shifted from port to starboard tanks, correcting the list of the ships for the time being.

Shells began to bracket the *Salt Lake City* as she slowed. Capt. Rodgers swung his ships sharply right, to 200° T., to avoid these salvos. Despite this momentary deviation from course, the ship continued to be subjected to the accurate fire of a heavy cruiser which bore 200° R. from her. By 1129, the oil and water in her after engine room were being pumped out and her after engines were being eased back into operation, but she was again listing to port.

Meantime, the screening destroyers had slowed, as they tried to keep position between the injured cruiser and the enemy. At 1129, in an attempt to open the range and throw off the enemy's fire control, Admiral McMorris set the group's course at 180° T. Our ships were now in formation with the *Richmond* in the van 6,000 yards ahead of the *Salt Lake City*, while the four destroyers were stationed off the stern of the heavy cruiser. The *Bailey* was about 1,500 yards off her starboard quarter, the *Coghlan* was approximately 3,000 yards dead astern, and the *Dale* and *Monaghan* were about 1,000 yards off the port quarter. From the *Dale,* the range to the nearest Japanese heavy cruiser was 18,000 yards. This ship, apparently of the *Nachi* class, bore 330° T. from our destroyer.

As the distance between Task Group Mike and the enemy grew smaller, Commander Task Group directed ComDesRon 14 to prepare to make a torpedo attack with the destroyers. This contemplated action was to provide cover for the retirement of the zigzagging *Salt Lake City* which, at 1132, was picking up additional speed on three engines.

At this time, our heavy cruiser was exchanging shots with a *Nachi* class heavy cruiser. That enemy ship, still on bearing 330° T., was also engaged by the *Dale* at a distance of 16,900 yards. The *Dale* ceased firing, however, when our destroyers began forming for their proposed attack.

The four destroyers increased their speed to 30 knots and formed up on heading 150° T. At 1134, however, the *Salt Lake City* requested Commander Task Group to designate one destroyer to stand by her for screening purposes; Admiral McMorris ordered ComDesRon 14 to detail a destroyer for this duty. Capt. Riggs received Admiral McMorris' message just after the destroyers made a left turn to an attack course of 060° T. The *Dale* promptly returned to base course, and continued laying smoke about the *Salt Lake City.*

The *Monaghan* had been listening to this exchange of orders and counterorders, and had failed to hear an acknowledgment of the screening assignment from the *Dale.* Fearing that the *Salt Lake City* would be left unguarded, the *Monaghan* informed ComDesRon 14 that she was still in position to lay smoke close by the heavy cruiser. Since no acknowledgment had been received from the *Dale,* Capt. Riggs countermanded his last order, and directed her to carry out the torpedo attack as originally scheduled. At the same time, he instructed the *Monaghan* to remain on station by the *Salt Lake City.*

Both the *Dale* and the *Monaghan* were now engaged in making smoke astern of the *Salt Lake City*. In the midst of the turmoil created by the billowing smoke and falling shells, each ship supposed that the other was standing in for the attack. Actually, only the *Bailey* and *Coghlan* were steaming forward on course 060° T. As they did so, Capt. Riggs, who thought he was leading three ships, announced: "The targets are the heavies." The enemy shifted his fire to the *Bailey* and *Coghlan*, scoring many near hits, as the range shortened.

Meanwhile, the *Salt Lake City* had been building up speed on three engines. At 1138, when she was making 26 knots, the destroyers' attack was no longer deemed necessary. Admiral McMorris ordered ComDesRon 14 to "belay the attack." Capt. Riggs immediately directed the destroyers to reform on our cruisers. Despite the cancellation, however, the feint toward the enemy had forced him to make a sharp turn to the right, thereby opening the range somewhat.

Task Group Mike continued southward on base course 180° T., with the Japanese force now headed generally southwestward. Firing was spasmodic, with all ships in our group loosing an occasional salvo at both heavy and light cruiser targets. Mean range was 18,000 yards, and the after guns were engaged almost exclusively. After reforming astern, our four destroyers again blanketed the *Salt Lake City* with smoke, but shells from the Japanese heavy cruisers landed close as the vessels steamed southward. Projectiles from one enemy salvo hit the water both over and short of the *Dale*, but she emerged unscathed.

Soon after 1140, word was passed aboard the *Salt Lake City* that ammunition for her after turrets was running low. Safety measures were abandoned in the face of necessity. Hatches were broken open, and shells from the forward ammunition stowage were trundled aft on dollies. Below deck, chains of men passed powder bags from the forward magazines to the after guns. Turret III ran out of AP ammunition before this powder-and-shell brigade could supply its guns, and some HC projectiles were fired. The shells burst with "terrific" detonations near the enemy ships, but it was impossible to judge the damage inflicted. The use of bombardment shells evidently led the enemy to think that an air attack was underway, for his heavy cruisers immediately opened a furious antiaircraft barrage into the overcast.

No sooner had the ammunition crisis been met, however, than a worse one developed. Sea water had been seeping into the fuel tanks aft as a result of hits taken there. This water contaminated the oil flowing to the burners, and the fires under the boilers went out, one by one. The *Salt Lake City* commenced dropping back, and the destroyers slowed to stay with her.

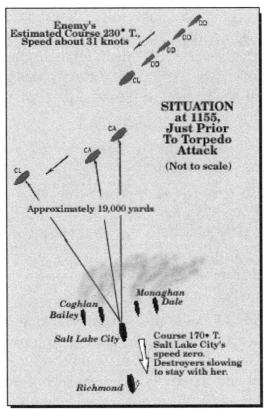

Situation at 1155, Just Prior to Torpedo Attack

It was at approximately 1147, when the group had swung left to 170° T., that our heavy cruiser's engines stopped. About this time she sent Admiral a message: "Have just received two hits broadside below the water line." Our ships made another ten degree left turn to 160° T. at 1149, when the *Salt Lake City's* momentum was carrying her along at about 13 knots. Many near hits struck the water close by our heavy cruiser and the screening destroyers, but there were no direct hits. At 1153 the speed of the *Salt Lake City* was eight knots. At 1155 it was zero.

The situation was dangerous. About 19,000 yards off the port quarter of the *Salt Lake City* were the two Japanese heavy cruisers. A light cruiser was approximately the same distance off her starboard quarter. These ships seemed to be closing. Because of the well-laid smoke screen, the enemy was unaware that our heavy cruiser had lost headway. However, this fact would soon become obvious. The *Salt Lake City* turned just before stopping, so that all her guns could bear for a last defense. She fired several full salvos while in this position, and at sometime during this period, "the enemy was kind enough to shoot an 8-inch shell through the zero flag" of the signal "My speed zero."

"Execute Torpedo Attack"

At 1155 Capt. Rodgers reported his ship's condition to Admiral McMorris. Commander Task Group promptly directed ComDesRon 14 to execute a covering torpedo attack on the Japanese force. Capt. Riggs immediately ordered the *Bailey, Coghlan,* and *Monaghan* to carry out the assault. The *Dale* was left to screen the *Salt Lake City.*

ComDesRon 14 told the three attacking destroyers to prepare their torpedoes, and designated "the two big boys" as the targets. The enemy was on an estimated course of 230° T., steaming at about 31 knots. The *Monaghan* ceased making smoke, and swerved right to cut across the bow of the *Salt Lake City.* To starboard of our heavy cruiser, the destroyer fell into column about 2,000 yards astern of the *Coghlan*, which was, in turn, some 600 yards behind the *Bailey*.

The three destroyers came right until they were on a torpedo firing course of 300° T. As they swung to this heading, the Japanese ships checked fire on the *Salt Lake City* and turned their guns on the smaller vessels. These ships answered with rapid fire from their forward guns. The *Bailey* chose the leading heavy cruiser as her target and commenced firing at three-second intervals. This ship was on bearing about 010° T. The *Coghlan* opened on the second heavy cruiser, which was in line behind the other heavy. The *Monaghan*, which was trying to close the *Coghlan*, first engaged the van heavy cruiser. As the range shortened, she shifted fire successively to the second heavy, and then to a light cruiser.

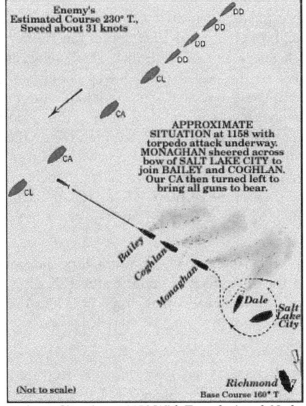

Approximate Situation at 1158 With Torpedo Attack Underway

Approximately 17,000 yards had separated the *Bailey* and the targets at the beginning of the run. This distance diminished rapidly as our ships zigzagged in to the attack. Spouts of water, some of which were tinted green or blue from dye-loaded shells, erupted on every side. All three destroyers were making smoke, the *Monaghan* having resumed at 1202. The *Coghlan* benefited by the smoke laid by the *Bailey,* while the *Monaghan,* last in line, was the most effectively covered of the three. To Admiral McMorris, the three ships appeared to be "smothered with splashes," as they steamed forward at maximum speed. "It was incredible that they should survive," he added, "but they continued in."

Accuracy of gunnery increased in direct ratio to the lessening range. Observers saw our destroyers score several hits on each heavy cruiser. A light cruiser also took at least one shell. The enemy's counterfire also grew more effective. Major and minor caliber shells straddled our ships continuously. None struck home, however, until 1203, when the *Bailey* took several hits in quick succession. One 8-inch shell penetrated inboard and exploded in the galley passageway. Fragments from this projectile completely wrecked the provision issuing room, while the concussion blew out bulkheads and tore doors off their hinges. One officer and three enlisted men were killed instantly, and four enlisted men were seriously wounded, one of them later dying. One officer and two enlisted men were slightly injured. The victims were members of repair parties who had gathered outside the galley to carry sandwiches to the gun crews.

Another 8-inch shell which hit at this time did not explode. It caromed off the after deck at about frame 172, digging a 6-inch gash in the deck before glancing off No. 4 mount and continuing on its way.

In addition the ship suffered damage from numerous near hits. Fragments struck the radio antenna, punctured the gig, and perforated the uptakes. On the starboard side, the skin of the ship was twisted and buckled at the waterline between frames 63 and 70.

When the *Bailey* sustained these hits, Capt. Riggs directed Lt. Comdr. Atkeson to fire his ship's torpedoes. ComDesRon 14 took this action with the realistic assumption that other shells would strike the van destroyer at any moment and render her unable to launch her torpedoes at all. Accordingly, at 1204, five torpedoes were expended. The target was the second heavy cruiser in line, range about 9,500 yards. All the torpedoes seemed to run hot, straight, and normal. A few minutes later, several observers on board the *Bailey* reported seeing "a large black column of what appeared to be oil and debris" rise abreast the mainmast of the target.

Unfortunately, Capt. Riggs' expectation was fulfilled a few seconds after the torpedoes were fired. The *Bailey* was hit by two 8-inch shell fragments at the same moment. One chunk of metal made a six-by-three-inch hole in the starboard side of the hull at frame 72 and entered the forward fireroom. This waterline perforation was plugged with mattresses and shored. Some flooding resulted from the hit, but pumps in the compartment controlled it. The other shell splinter ripped a jagged hole, six inches by twenty inches, in the hull at frame 101 starboard, entering the forward engine room. Repair parties were hampered in their efforts to close this hole, because it was in an almost inaccessible spot just outboard of the fuel oil purifier pump. Water began to pour in.

Immediately after launching the torpedoes, Lt. Comdr. Atkeson swung the *Bailey* hard left for retirement. Her gyro, radar, and sound gear were out of operation.

As the *Bailey* came about, the *Coghlan* and *Monaghan*, which had been following in her wake, also turned sharply left. Neither ship launched torpedoes because the range was extreme and the Japanese cruisers were heading northwestward, away from the direction of the attack.

As the *Coghlan* heeled over in her turn, several explosions close aboard "sprayed shrapnel on topside." Flying pieces of steel holed the stack in several places, pierced the bridge, put both the SC and FD radars out of action, and caused other relatively minor damage. Fragments seriously injured the executive officer, and inflicted minor wounds on two enlisted men. The *Monaghan*, farthest from the enemy and somewhat better covered by smoke, was not damaged.

While the destroyers were carrying out their attack, the *Salt Lake City* had got underway. Her forward engines began turning over slowly at 1158, after she had lain dead in the water for three minutes. At the same time, Capt. Rodgers ordered fire checked, in order to conserve ammunition "for a final attack on the closing Japanese force." Once the ship's inertia was overcome, however, speed was built up quickly. By 1200 she was making 15 knots. At 1202, when it became clear that a reserve of ammunition for a last defense was unnecessary, her after guns again opened on the enemy. The *Salt Lake City's* last salvo of the battle was fired by turret III at 1204. The *Dale*, which had been laying smoke and shooting at the enemy at the same time, ceased fire at 1205.

Meanwhile the *Richmond* had drawn ahead some distance to the south. About 1200, she turned left and steamed back to cover the *Salt Lake City* and the retiring destroyers. She began making smoke at 1207, but desisted at 1211 when the enemy force was seen definitely to be on a westward course.

The Retirement

As our three destroyers stood southeastward to rejoin the remainder of the task group, the *Bailey* began to experience the effects of the hits she had taken. Efforts to stop the flow of water into the forward engine room had been futile. High speeds caused water to spurt into the ship with a force which literally swept men off their feet. Fire and bilge pumps proved inadequate, and the water level rose fast.

Although the lubricating oil by-pass to the main circulating pump was ruptured, it was decided to use that pump as long as possible to prevent the flooding of the engine room. This action succeeded in holding the water level down, while further endeavors were made to plug the breach in the hull. After the pump had operated for a few minutes, however, the oil pressure gauge began to drop. Attempts were made to shift to the electric standby pump, but spray had short-circuited the power panel and this pump could not be started. Sparks began to fly from the overheated main engine bearings, and the entire ship began to shake. Steam lines vibrated as much as six inches, but held up under the strain. The water level rose steadily. It was decided to abandon the forward engine room. Boilers No. 1 and No. 2 and pumps in the compartment were secured, and the room was vacated. Although the *Bailey* began to slow gradually after the starboard engine ceased operating at 1207, she was still making 25 knots at 1209.

By this time, the *Salt Lake City* had succeeded in lighting off all her boilers. She was making approximately 17 knots on course 140° T., despite an eight or nine degree list to port. All firing had ceased by 1212, when Admiral McMorris changed the group's course to 090° T. Speed was set at 18 knots. The gradually accelerating *Salt Lake City* was capable of exceeding that speed by then, however, and she went to 24 knots in order to close the flagship. At 1215 our heavy cruiser's speed dropped to 22 knots when the electric submersible pumps in the after engine room broke down. Repair parties began overhauling the equipment immediately, in a race against the rising water in the compartment.

At 1224, shortly after ComDesRon 14 had reported that the *Bailey* could make 24 knots on her one operative engine, the *Salt Lake City* informed Commander Task Group that her speed had been reduced to 20 knots, a figure she hoped to maintain.

The *Monaghan,* whose starboard reduction gear was still making grating noises, also encountered further engineering difficulties at this time. Steam lines on her No. 1 and No. 2 fuel oil service pumps were carried away, and her maximum speed was temporarily reduced to 24 knots. Admiral McMorris had set 20 knots as the speed for the task group immediately after receiving the *Salt Lake City's* message. He did not learn of the *Monaghan's* troubles until some time later.

By 1226, the *Salt Lake City* was squared away on base course, making 23 knots to close the *Richmond*. The enemy was moving off to the west, and the personnel aboard our heavy cruiser expressed themselves also as being in favor of "getting the hell out of here."

About this time, complications developed in the after engine room of the *Bailey*. Steam and water vapor filled the compartment, and safety valves began popping in the after fireroom. It was hard to determine the exact cause of the difficulty in the foggy compartment, but since the main feed water pumps seemed to be at fault, they were secured. The ship came to a complete standstill at 1230, while a changeover to emergency feed was effected. After a four-minute interval, the *Bailey* again picked up way. A broken feed water pressure line, the cause of the trouble, was quickly located and shut off. Main feed pressure was then restored, and by 1235 the ship was making 15 knots on the port engine.

No sooner was the ship under way, however, than further difficulties beset her. The after main switchboard, which had been drenched with water, short-circuited. All electric power on the ship was lost. Steering was shifted to hand power, and guns and directors switched to local control.

At 1235, the *Coghlan,* which had been ordered to stand by, ceased making smoke, slowed to 20 knots, and circled back to the *Bailey*. The *Monaghan,* which had stopped laying smoke a few minutes earlier, was directed to rejoin the cruisers.

Task Group Mike's speed was reduced to 15 knots at 1239, so that the *Bailey* would not be left too far astern. The group's other cripple, the *Salt Lake City,* now had the flooding in her after engine room under control, and had closed to within a few thousand yards of the *Richmond,* which was in latitude 53°10′ N., longitude 167°30′ E. Since none of her gyros was functioning, our heavy cruiser stayed on course by following the flagship's movements.

At 1240, in response to a request from the task group commander, ComDesRon 14 reported that the enemy was about 42,000 yards from the *Bailey,* bearing 275° T. A suggestion by Capt. Riggs that he take two destroyers and trail the Japanese force was vetoed by Admiral McMorris. At 1244, a few moments after the *Dale* and *Bailey* had ceased making smoke, Admiral McMorris asked Capt. Riggs to keep him advised of the enemy's movements. ComDesRon 14 informed him that the Japanese force had disappeared over the horizon to the west.

When the *Coghlan* maneuvered into position close by the *Bailey* at 1245, she stopped all her engines and prepared to take the damaged destroyer in tow. By that time, however, the *Bailey* was forging ahead on base course 090° T. She had recovered use of her gyro and, although her speed fluctuated, it was decided that towing was unnecessary. The *Coghlan* followed her closely, however, and relayed messages back and forth between the *Bailey* and the task group commander. This arrangement was necessary because all power was still out on the destroyer flagship.

At 1251, the *Salt Lake City's* SC radar picked up a surface contact bearing 126° R., distant 20,000 yards. This pip faded away after remaining on the screen for five minutes.

Our ships began to assume a cruising disposition as they continued eastward. Both the *Richmond* and *Salt Lake City* started zigzagging according to plan. The heavy cruiser, the forward gyros of which were back in operation, was about 1,500 yards astern of the flagship. The *Dale* moved up and took station as antisubmarine screen 2,000 yards off the starboard bow of the *Richmond.* Shortly thereafter, the *Monaghan* assumed a similar position off the port bow of the light cruiser.

The *Coghlan* and *Bailey* closed the other ships slowly. At 1303 fire broke out in the uptake vent of the *Coghlan's* No. 2 stack. At 1311, while repair parties were battling the blaze, an enemy float plane was sighted to starboard. The *Coghlan's* 40-mm. guns opened at a range of about 9,000 yards, and the scout banked away undamaged. This aircraft continued to shadow the formation for some time, with the *Salt Lake City* making numerous contacts on it, both visual and radar.

The fire aboard the *Coghlan* was extinguished at 1316. Eight minutes later the *Bailey's* gyro again became inoperative. No further casualties occurred, however, and at 1335 an attempt was made to correct the destroyer flagship's starboard list. Fresh water was shifted from starboard to port tanks, and the starboard depth charges were jettisoned. All were carefully set on safe before being tossed overboard; nevertheless one exploded. These measures rectified the ship's list somewhat, although she still had a slow rolling motion in the water.

While the *Bailey* and *Coghlan* were thus occupied, the *Salt Lake City* again picked up what was though to be a surface contact. The pip on her SG radar screen bore 110° R., distant 20,000 yards. Before the heavy cruiser could get the information through to the task group commander via TBS, the contact faded. At 1340, Admiral McMorris, having seen the heavy cruiser's flag hoist, inquired as to whether the contact had been on a surface craft or a plane. When told that it was on a ship, he asked whether or not anything was in sight and, if so, on what bearing. The pertinent data was given, and it was explained that visual contact had not been established. Thereafter, the *Salt Lake City* made other radar contacts until, at 1350, it was decided that the pip on her screen represented an aircraft instead of a vessel. At 1405 the troublesome contact was finally sighted. It proved to be a PBY. By 1418, three of our patrol planes were over the area.

As time passed, the *Bailey* and *Coghlan* rejoined the group and our ships continued their retirement to the eastward. It became apparent that further contact with the enemy during the remaining hours of daylight was unlikely. Guns were unloaded through the muzzle, and temporary repairs were effected. The *Salt Lake City* jettisoned several hundred rounds of 40-mm. ammunition. Blast from the 8-inch guns in turrets III and IV had damaged these shells, and also had done considerable injury to the 40-mm. mounts, directors, and shields. More than a thousand rounds of 5-inch common and illuminating shells were also lost because of the flooding in the after 5-inch magazine and handling room.

Admiral McMorris, early in the afternoon, had sent a summary of the battle to Admiral Kinkaid. The task group commander informed the task force commander that it was his tentative plan to have the *Salt Lake City* and *Bailey* proceed to Adak, while the other ships headed for the approaches to Holtz Bay to intercept the enemy if he should make another attempt to reach his base at Attu. However, Admiral Kinkaid's return message assured Admiral McMorris that if the Japanese force had not withdrawn, submarines and aircraft would take up the battle against it. The task force commander detailed two additional destroyers to join the task group on the morning of the 27th, and said that he would arrange for air cover for the group. He directed all ships to put in at Adak.

At 1604, U.S. Army planes, three B-25 bombers and eight P-38 fighters, were sighted in latitude 53° N., longitude 186°40′ E. These aircraft, which had left Amchitka at 1330, had been delayed because it had been necessary to install an extra fuel tank in each of them. While they were en route to the battle area, PBYs made contact with the two enemy merchant vessels some distance to the northwest of our force. These patrol planes carried no bombs, but they maintained contact until 1630, transmitting directions for the Army bombers. Lack of fuel made it impossible for the Army aircraft to act on the information, and they returned to their base.

At 1702, while Task Group Mike was in latitude 52°53′ N., longitude 169°53′ E., 13 B-24s and 8 B-25s were sighted. These planes had left Adak at 1336 to attack the enemy force.

However, shortly after they passed over our ships, a Catalina reported that the Japanese group was more than 100 miles farther east. Again a shortage of gasoline prevented our Army aircraft from striking. The planes flew back to Adak.

Admiral Kinkaid modified his orders to Task Group Mike later in the day, and the *Salt Lake City, Coghlan,* and *Monaghan* went directly to Dutch Harbor, where they arrived on the 29th. The *Richmond, Bailey,* and *Dale,* accompanied by the destroyers *Dewey* and *Caldwell* (Lt. Comdr. Horatio A. Lincoln) which joined early on the 27th, put in at Kuluk Bay, Adak, about 0200 on the 28th.

Observations

The Battle of the Komandorskis lasted almost three and one-half hours, and was our longest daylight surface engagement of the war up to that time. It was an action at extended range — by necessity on our part, by choice on the part of the Japanese. Our initial stab at the enemy's auxiliaries was promptly and effectively blocked by his combatant ships. Thereafter, as our cruisers were outnumbered two to one, Task Group Mike maneuvered discreetly to keep the range open as far as possible, while trying to inflict as much damage as it could on the enemy. If our force had succeeded in knocking out one or two of the Japanese ships, as appeared possible at times during the battle, Task Group Mike could have tried to fight its way around the rest of the combatant ships to chase the fleeing auxiliaries, or it could have closed the crippled men-o'-war to administer the *coup de grace,* whichever seemed more feasible. Since this desirable state of affairs did not come about, our ships had no choice but to keep the Japanese at arm's length. The enemy, on the other hand, with his advantages in numbers and firepower, made no serious, concerted attempt to close with our weaker force. In the words of Admiral McMorris, "He seemed to be content to fight a duel using his heavy cruisers."

The singular reluctance of the Japanese to employ their destroyers during the action aroused much speculation among the officers of our group. Experience with the enemy in the South Pacific has shown that he is skillful in the use of his light forces. Perhaps his wariness was dictated by reason of the load the destroyers may have carried — troops, ammunition, or vital supplies. Because the Japanese customarily used destroyers for these purposes in the Solomon Islands it is easy to believe that they were on a similar mission on this occasion.

Since the *Salt Lake City* was the recipient of most of the enemy's attentions, that ship probably is the best authority on details of Japanese gunnery. The following quotation is from our heavy cruiser's report:

"Two CA's maintained a heavy, deliberate and concentrated fire on the *Salt Lake City* throughout . . . One cruiser, using a bilious green dye, was relatively ineffective. The other cruiser, using blue dye exactly like our own, became very effective It is estimated that this CA contributed most of the 200 rounds which fell within 50 yards of this ship. Patterns of both ships were excellent, with a maximum dispersion of 200 yards by 30 yards. Also, they checked fire when we were hidden by smoke and very methodically opened with extremely close salvos when we came into view. This indicates very deliberate firing. Shells fell with a high angle of fall, causing noticeably small splashes, with the shells detonating well below the surface of the water."

Because of the heavy smoke screen and the long ranges at which the battle was fought, detailed results of our gunnery could not be ascertained. The fact that both Japanese heavy cruisers were firing at a reduced rate during the later part of the engagement suggests that our gunfire may have caused heavier damage than was apparent. A depleted ammunition supply probably was another contributory factor in this slackening of fire.

The remarkably few hits sustained by our ships bring out the relative ineffectiveness of the enemy's plane spotting.

however, it was the unanimous opinion of those who commented on the battle that range spots furnished by cruiser aircraft would have been helpful to our ships. Admiral McMorris, in his report says: "Looking backwards, it is now felt that the advantages of employing them would have outweighed the disadvantages involved."

All personnel conducted themselves in a highly creditable manner. The officers and men who participated in the torpedo attack were singled out for special praise by Admiral McMorris. He termed our destroyers' exploit "a magnificent and inspiring spectacle." Repair parties aboard our damaged ships acted coolly and efficiently, and made a real contribution to the successful outcome of the battle by keeping the effects of the hits to a minimum. Gun crews also turned in an outstanding piece of work. The *Salt Lake City* was able to hold her own in an 8-inch gun duel with the two Japanese heavy cruisers because of the tireless work of the personnel assigned to her after turrets. For the greater part of the engagement, the officers and men at the No. 3 and No. 4 guns aboard our destroyers labored unfailingly in the acrid fumes of the smoke which steamed from the stacks of those ships. During the heat of battle, at least one convert to frequent gun drill was made. One of the *Dale's* men was heard to remark fervently that he "wouldn't mind all the loading drill any more."

Conclusions

"The Komandorski action was well fought. It resulted in turning back a decidedly superior enemy force escorting two transports or cargo ships, thereby preventing reinforcements of either personnel or material from reaching enemy held island in the Aleutians. This result constituted an important contribution, of far reaching importance, in the North Pacific campaign." Thus Admiral Kinkaid summarized the Battle of the Komandorskis.

Summary of Ammunition Expended

Caliber	Salt Lake City	Richmond	Bailey	Coghlan	Monaghan	Dale	Totals
8"/55 AP	806						806
8"/55 HC	26						26
6"/47 Common & Dye loaded		271					271
5"/38 Common			482	750	201	364	1,797
5"/38 Dye loaded					2	80	82
5"/38 AA Common					32	284	316
5"/25 AA Common	95						95
3"/50 AA		24					24
40-mm.					48		48
Totals	927	295	482	750	283	728	3,465

Chapter 10: Second Bombardment of Attu
26 April 1943

During March our air operations had been stepped up to an extent which permitted 39 raids to be made on Kiska during the month. In early April, however, a spell of stormy weather with winds up to 108 m.p.h. grounded all planes for five days. Nevertheless, by the 21st Kiska had been attacked 83 times, and by the end of the month 640 tons of bombs had been dropped.

Meanwhile strong reinforcements for the North Pacific Force began to reach the area in preparation for the eventual assault on Attu. These included two battleships, four cruisers, and many destroyers. Admiral McMorris' striking group had lost the services of the *Salt Lake City, Bailey, Dale,* and *Monaghan,* but had been strengthened by the assignment of the *Santa Fe* (Capt. Russel S. Berkey), *Detroit* (Capt. Ellis H. Beiselman), *Bancroft* (Comdr. John L. Melgaard), *Caldwell* (Lt. Comdr. Horatio A Lincoln), *Edwards* (Lt. Comdr. Paul G. Osler), *Frazier* (Lt. Comdr. Frank Virden), and *Gansevoort* (Comdr. Edward A. McFall). During April it operated westward and northwestward of Attu, to prevent supplies and reinforcements reaching the western islands. The last ship known to have reached Attu was the *Kankyo Maru* (3,200 tons) which arrived and departed on 25 March. It is believed that after the Battle of the Komandorskis no enemy ships, except submarines, ran the blockade, but there was the continuing threat that the attempt would be made.

Task Group Mike was conducting its usual patrol on the afternoon of 25 April when it received a dispatch from Admiral Kinkaid directing the bombardment of Holtz Bay and Chichagof Harbor shortly after daylight the next day. Preparations were immediately made and targets assigned to individual ships. Course was laid for Holtz Bay and a speed of 20 knots set to arrive off its entrance soon after daybreak.

About 0530 Attu was sighted to the southeastward. Visibility was poor, with fog patches and snow squalls in many directions. An hour later the weather was still unpromising. Wind and sea had picked up so much that the contemplated launching of aircraft was canceled, since recovery would have been most hazardous. At this time heading was changed to 130° T., the bombardment course, which was maintained thereafter except for a six-minute interval when the group shifted course to close the coastline.

The weather began to clear slightly at 0800. Fifteen minutes later signal to commence firing was executed. The order of ships was *Caldwell, Bancroft, Coghlan, Richmond, Santa Fe, Detroit, Frazier*, Gansevoort, and *Edwards*. To avoid interfering with each other's fire, ships were, for the most part, to fire in succession, though not necessarily in accordance with their positions in the column.

The *Caldwell* began the action. The *Santa Fe* then joined in, and after several minutes a mass of black, smoke was observed in the east arm of Holtz Bay, near the airfield. At 0830 a small fog patch drifted across the harbor entrance and prevented firing for a short interval. When the guns resumed, various conflagrations and explosions were noted, but none of any great importance. By 0840 signal was made to cease firing, since allotted ammunition had been expended, and the headlands were closing off all targets. At the end of the bombardment, air coverage was instituted by a B-24 and later by a patrol plane.

Better results might have been achieved, in the opinion of Admiral McMorris, if it had been possible to use spotting planes. But the task group commander feared that the harbors would soon be completely closed down by the fog and felt that he should make use of present opportunities. As it was, except for the lack of spotting aircraft, "conditions proved to be excellent." The task group commander believed that the bombardment had been much more effective than the previous one of 18 February. Fire control was generally satisfactory.

No major installations or shipping were observed. There were no signs of personnel or activity ashore. A number of small buildings and huts, however, testified to the presence of the enemy, even if he did not choose to give away the positions of his artillery by firing on the task group. In April the task group was familiar with the area and was augmented by the *Santa Fe*, a most effective bombardment ships. Photographs taken nine or ten days after the action showed many craters in regions where building activity had been noted by prior reconnaissance, as well as in the vicinity of the incomplete airfield. In view of later experience, however, it seems unlikely that a restricted bombardment of this type could have caused more than transitory inconvenience to the enemy.

By the end of April, Adak, the center of operations in the Aleutians area, was maintaining a garrison of 19,067 Army personnel and 7,811 Navy. At Amchitka, where there were 10,260 Army and 903 Navy personnel, a 5,000-foot bomber strip had been completed during the month. The new fields on Amchitka enabled our air power at last to assume significant proportions. Many buildings in the Main Camp area on Kiska, as well as part of the submarine base, had been destroyed. But despite the 1,000 sorties made by our planes during April, new construction on Kiska and Attu rapidly replaced damaged structures.

In May we made 35 strikes in 22 days, 17 against Kiska, 17 against Attu, and one directed at the Rat Islands. Our air forces dropped 470 tons of bombs on the two major islands with a loss of 28 planes, only three of which were known to have been destroyed by enemy action. But in this month air activity was suddenly eclipsed by the long-hoped-for, long-planned invasion of Attu.

Chapter 11: The Invasion of Attu
May 1943

Planning and Training

Early in the Aleutians Campaign, Kiska came to be regarded as the primary objective in our reconquest of the enemy-held islands. Not only was it the most advanced Japanese threat to those Aleutians remaining in our possession and to the Alaskan mainland, but it provided better potential air facilities, a more satisfactory harbor, and terrain more suitable for a base.

Consequently, in December 1942, Rear Admiral Francis W. Rockwell, Commander Amphibious Force Pacific Fleet (and later ComTaskFor Roger), was directed by CINCPAC to submit an estimate of the situation and a plan for the reduction and occupation of Kiska. Admiral Rockwell in turn called upon Maj. Gen. Holland M. Smith, USMC, commanding Amphibious Corps Pacific Fleet, for his judgment as to the forces required and for a tactical plan. Since available information was insufficient, General Smith was unable to submit a tactical plan, but he believed that about 27,000 men would be required, an estimate which closely approximated those reached independently by Admiral Nimitz and Admiral Kinkaid, Command North Pacific and Commander Task Force King (formerly Task Force Tare).

Early in January CINCPAC forwarded to ComTaskFor Roger and ComTaskFor King a plan developed jointly with Lt. Gen. John L. DeWitt, Commanding General Western Defense Command, which provided for training a force for the assault upon and occupation of Kiska. Army forces were to include the 7th Infantry Division plus the 184th Infantry Regiment, the 507th AA Regiment, and part of the Alaska garrison force. The training staff, transports, and landing craft were to be supplied by Task Force Roger. Support ships were to be provided by CINCPAC, since Task Force King still contained only a few cruisers and destroyers. Training of units in the United States proper was to be conducted under the supervision of Task Force Roger and the Western Defense Command at Fort Ord, California, while the Alaskan units, although indirectly under the same control, were actually to be trained by Task Force King and the Alaska Defense Command. The four commanders were to form a joint staff for training and for the conduct of the operation itself.

Shortly thereafter, Maj. Gen. A.E. Brown, USA, reported to ComTaskFor Roger with the 7th Infantry Division, reinforced, which was placed in training at Fort Ord under Maj. Gen. Smith. By 15 January preliminary work had begun, but until 10 February the division was at only about 70 per cent strength. Initial instruction was given by Marine officers. On 24 January Admiral Rockwell reported to CINCPAC that the earliest date of troop readiness would be about 1 May, assuming that four attack transports and one attack cargo vessel were available on 22 February and an additional division of ships a week later.

By the end of January the joint staff had assembled in San Diego and begun detailed study of the forthcoming operation. Basic decisions were reached regarding equipment and personnel desired, and resulting recommendations were closely followed, except as modified by circumstances and the non-availability of some items.

Early in February available shipping suffered a reduction because of other commitments, and COMINCH directed that preparations for the Kiska operation be modified accordingly. A revised estimate of required forces was to be submitted after the results of the current air offensive based on Amchitka were known. Shortly thereafter it was necessary to withdraw all AKAs and all but two APAs from training use because of combat needs. Instruction of the 7th Division continued as best it could, however, in order to capitalize on whatever results the air attacks from Amchitka might produce.

Amphibious training of that portion of the invasion force already in Alaska presented its own difficulties. No proper equipment was on hand, nor could a sufficient number of officer instructors be detached for duty in the north. It was suggested that key personnel be brought from Alaska to Fort Ord for training, but the Army proved unable to act on this recommendation.

The first actual landing exercises were conducted in California between 21 February and 9 March, using the two remaining APAs. Combat loading, embarkation, debarkation, ship-to-shore movements, rubber boat training, and boat gun firing were stressed.

Two more APAs, the *Zeilin* and *Heywood,* were then added to the two already on hand (*J. Franklin Bell* and *Harris*). With these four ships and the XAP *President Fillmore* further exercises were held between 17 and 27 March. Included was a daylight landing on San Clemente Island, with actual gunfire support by the battleships *Idaho, Nevada,* and *Pennsylvania* and the destroyers *Abner Read* (Comdr. Thomas Burrowes), *Doyle* (Lt. Comdr. Clarence E. Boyd), *MacDonough,* and *Phelps.* Carrier Aircraft Composite Squadrons 13 and 20 dropped live bombs and strafed with live ammunition. After the troops were reembarked, the combatant vessels engaged in a series of firing exercises in which call fire was delivered in response to requests by shore fire control parties.

The shortage of troop equipment and the lack of AKAs unfortunately prevented full scale loading for the exercises. It was difficult, therefore, to indoctrinate properly the personnel of shore parties attached to the regimental landing groups. The air squadrons employed were not those which were to support the landing, since these were already in the area, carrying on the offensive from Amchitka. Consequently the latter planes received no training in amphibious operations or in direct support of ground troops.

The shortage of equipment and shipping was such that on 3 March Admiral Kinkaid recommended that the Kiska operation be tabled for the time being, and that an attack on Attu be substituted. Upon request from CINCPAC for additional details, Admiral Kinkaid submitted a brief estimate, including the following points:

(a) Probable Japanese garrison, 500 men.
(b) Only artillery defenses, a few AA guns.
(c) Capture could probably be effected by one reinforced infantry regiment, plus the 7th Division's mountain artillery.
(d) Only four APAs and two or three AKAs required.
(e) Three or four cruisers, two or three battleships, and two squadrons of destroyers would suffice for escort, bombardment, and covering force.
(f) Seabees or Army engineers could construct a landing strip on nearby Shemya Island in three weeks (more favorable terrain and weather than on Attu).

The Commanding General, Alaska Defense Command (Maj. Gen. Simon B. Buckner) concurred in general with these suggestions.

As a result, CINCPAC directed Admiral Rockwell to plan an operation against Attu. The joint staff discontinued work on the Kiska plan and began a study of the new objective. Training continued under the supervision of Admiral Rockwell, while

Admiral Kinkaid was designated to take command of the operation as a whole. On 11 March CINCPAC made the following surface forces available for the assault, support, and covering operations: three battleships, three heavy cruisers, three over-age light cruisers, one escort carrier, nineteen destroyers, plus tenders, oilers, mine-sweepers, etc., and four attack transports. No AKAs could be provided without taking them from the South Pacific, and this was disapproved. One XAP, the *Perida,* eventually accompanied the Force, carrying one LCM(3) and ten LCVs.

News that the Joint Chiefs of Staff were definitely committed to the operation was received by Admiral Rockwell on 24 March. On 1 April CINCPAC and General DeWitt issued the following joint directive:

"The objective is the reduction and occupation of Attu and the occupation of the most suitable airfield site in the Near Islands at the earliest practicable date. The purpose is to sever enemy lines of communication to the Western Aleutians, to deny the Near Islands to the enemy, and to construct an airfield thereon for air operations; to render Kiska untenable and to create a base of operations for possible future reduction and occupation of Kiska. The first task is to reduce and occupy the most suitable airfield site in the Near Islands and build an airfield thereon. Commander Task Force [KING] is in supreme command. Commander Amphibious Force, Pacific Fleet, is to operate under Commander Task Force [KING] and command amphibious operations until landing phase completed. The Army commander is Commanding General 7th Division. . . . The forces assigned Navy are Task Forces [KING] and [ROGER]. Army forces, assault, reserve, and initial occupation troops as follows: Assault on Attu, 7th Division Combat Team, consisting 17th Infantry, one battalion field artillery, one battalion engineers for shore parties, one battery AA automatic weapons, three detachments 75th Special Signal Company, one company 7th Division Organic Combat Engineers, one medical collecting company, 7th Division. One platoon 7th Division Medical

Clearing Company, Detachment Headquarters 7th Division Battalion, detachment 7th Division Quartermaster Battalion, detachment 7th Division Organic Signal Company. For the initial occupation of the selected site in the Near Islands, 18th Combat Engineers from Adak, 4th Infantry Composite Regiment from Adak. The floating reserve is one regimental combat team consisting of the 32nd Infantry with reinforcements similar to those for the 17th Infantry indicated above. The garrisons for Attu and the selected site in the Near Islands are to be designated by the Commanding General Western Defense Command, and are to include 17th Infantry Combat Team, 32nd Infantry Combat Team, 78th CAAA and 2nd Battalion 51st CAAA. The target date is May 7th, 1943. Command of occupied area will revert to the Army when senior Army officer Near Islands informs Commander Task Force [KING] that Army is ready to take over."

One auxiliary carrier, the *Nassau* (Capt. Austin K. Doyle), had been assigned to the operation, but because of the necessity for repairs, she did not become available until 16 April. Her squadron was organized subsequent to the assignment of the ships and had only five days to train. In general, the air plan was as follows: the carrier aircraft were primarily for air cover, but available for support if required. General air support was to be provided by the 11th Air Force, while long-range search was to be taken care of by PatWing Four. Spotting was to be carried out by ship-based seaplanes. The Army Air Force member of the joint staff was to be airborne at the scene of operations to coordinate Army air support. One Army-Navy liaison party was to accompany each battalion, as well as Commander Landing Force.

None of the personnel had had previous experience in this work. The *Nassau* squadron's limited training was cut short by the fact that weather prevented any launchings between the time of departure from the West Coast and D-day.

The plan for the capture of Attu included the use of scouts who were to be landed by dark in advance of the main assault.

Considerable delay was experienced in obtaining for this purpose the services of the submarines *Narwhal* (Lt. Comdr. Frank D. Latta) and *Nautilus* (Lt. Comdr. William H. Brockman, Jr.). The commanding officer of the Scout Company, 7th Division, and about 100 troops were given a limited period of training in the *Narwhal* off San Clemente Island before departure for Dutch Harbor on 18 April. The *Nautilus* was under repair at Pearl Harbor, and had to proceed directly to Dutch Harbor on 21 April. Her complement of scouts was sent north in transports and received brief training at Dutch Harbor before the sailing date of the expedition.

Before the APAs were sent to San Francisco to load the assault force, a general conference was held, attended by the transport commander (Capt. Pat Buchanan) and his staff, all commanding officers of APAs, and all transport quartermasters. At this meeting final discussions were held in connection with loading plans. Because of the lack of AKAs, the logistical problem was abnormally difficult, which resulted in considerable overloading of transport with both troops and cargo.

The APAs *Harris, Heywood, J. Franklin Bell,* and *Zeilin* arrived at San Francisco and began stowing cargo on 19 April. Soon they were joined by the motorship *Perida.* The loading was complete on 24 April, and the group departed for next day's rendezvous with the Naval Attack Force Commander (Admiral Rockwell). The latter had left San Pedro in the *Pennsylvania* on 23 April and had already rendezvoused with the *Nassau, Neches,* and screen. On the 25th the complete force set course for Cold Bay.

In order to maintain the utmost security concerning the planned assault, a number of effective measures had been adopted. A complete training order issued prior to departure from San Diego indicated that the force was merely going to train in that area. Medical officers were directed to give lecture on tropical diseases and on hygiene and sanitation in the tropics. Winter clothing shipped to the various vessels was concealed. After the rendezvous off San Francisco, the secret was finally divulged.

During the planning phase, all aspects of security were rigorously enforced. When plans were completed, a minute inspection of the office which had been used was made by the security officer. Each desk drawer was pulled open and the space back of it searched. Everything, including walls and floors, was gone over several times to make sure nothing was left.

During passage, conferences took place between associated echelons of the transport group and the landing force. All instruction feasible on shipboard was given. Photographs and relief maps were studied and the features of the terrain were discussed in detail.

While at anchor in Cold Bay on 1 May, debarkation drills were held. Debarkation and loading for the first boat trip were practiced the next day. A rehearsal landing which had been planned for the 3d, however, was abandoned because of dirty weather. All other drills were hampered by the necessary assignment of boats to other ships and by many special boat trips.

Simultaneously, joint Army-Navy conferences were held at which the final details of the task were worked out. D-day was tentatively set for 7 May, with H-hour at 0740. The basic plan for the operation had been prepared by the joint staff in San Diego.

The Western Defense Command estimated that enemy strength on Attu was now at least 1,350, mostly AA personnel and labor troops probably equipped as infantry. Admiral Kinkaid's estimate was 1,587.

As the Attack Force prepared to sail on its mission, the basic organization of Task Forces King and Roger was as follows:

Task Force King, Rear Admiral Thomas C. Kinkaid.

(a) *Shore-Based Air Group,* Maj. Gen. William O. Butler:

(1) Air Striking Unit, Maj. Gen. William O. Butler: 24 heavy bombers, 30 medium bombers, 128 fighters.

(2) Air Search Unit, Capt. Leslie E. Gehres: 24 PV-1s, 30 PBY-5As, 5 seaplane tenders.

(b) *Alaska Sector Escort and Supply Group,* Rear Admiral John W. Reeves, Jr.:

1 DD, 1 DMS, 1 DM, 2 DEs (Canadian), 1 PG, 3 AMs, 1 ATF, 4 LSTs, 8 LCT(5)s, miscellaneous small craft.

(c) *Motor Torpedo Boat Group*

11 MTBs.

(d) *Submarine Group.*

(e) *Southern Covering Group,* Rear Admiral Charles H. McMorris:

3 CLs:

Detroit, Capt. Ellis H. Beiselman.
Richmond, Capt. Theodore M. Waldschmidt.
Santa Fe, Capt. Russell S. Berkey.

5 DDs:

Bancroft, Comdr. John L. Melgaard.
Caldwell, Lt. Comdr. Horatio A. Lincoln.
Coghlan, Comdr. Benjamin F. Tompkins.
Frazier, Lt. Comdr. Frank Virden.
Gansevoort, Lt. Comdr. Montgomery L. McCullough, Jr.

(f) *Northern Covering Group,* Rear Admiral Robert C. Giffen.

3 CAs:

Louisville, Capt. Charles T. Joy.
San Francisco, Capt. Albert F. France.
Wichita, (F), Capt. John J. Mahoney.

4 DDs:

Balch, Comdr. Harold H. Tiemroth.
Hughes, Lt. Comdr. Herbert H. Marable.

Morris, Lt. Comdr. Edward S. Burns.
Mustin, Lt. Comdr. Earl T. Schreiber.

(g) *Attu Reinforcement Group,* Capt. Charles L. Hutton, USN:

32nd Infantry Regiment, less one battalion, embarked in 1 AP, 4 XAPs, 3 XAKs.

(h) *Tanker and Service Group:*

6 AOs:

Brazos, Comdr. Richard P. Glass.
Cuyama, Capt. Paul R. Coloney.
Guadalupe, Comdr. Herbert A. Anderson.
Neches, Comdr. Campbell D. Emory.
Platte, Comdr. Harry Keeler, Jr.
Tippecanoe, Comdr. Ralph O. Myers.

2 ADs:

Black Hawk, Comdr. Edward H. McMenemy.
Markab, Capt. Allen D. Brown.

(i) *Shemya Occupation Group,* Brig. Gen. John E. Copeland:
4th Infantry Regiment, 18th Engineer Regiment, to be transported in 1 AP, 1 XAP, 3 XAPc's, 1 XAK.

Task Force Roger (Attack Force), Rear Admiral Francis W. Rockwell.

(j) *Support Group*

3 BBs, Rear Admiral Howard F. Klingman:

Pennsylvania, (FF), Capt. William A. Corn.
Idaho, (F), Capt. Horace D. Clarke.
Nevada, Capt. William A. Kitts, III.

1 ACV:

Nassau, Capt. Austin K. Doyle

7 DDs:

Aylwin, Lt. Comdr. Ray E. Malpass.
Edwards, Lt. Comdr. Paul G. Osler.
Hull, Lt. Comdr. Andrew L. Young, Jr.

MacDonough, Lt. Comdr. Erle V.E. Dennett.
Meade, Comdr. Raymond S. Lamb.
Monaghan, Lt. Comdr. Peter H. Horn.
Phelps, Lt. Comdr. John E. Edwards (F, Capt. Ruthven E. Libby, ComDesRon One and Commander Screening Group).

(k) *Transport Group*, Capt. Pat Buchanan:

4 APA:

J. Franklin Bell, Comdr. John B. McGovern.
Harris, Comdr. Albert M. Van Eaton.
Heywood, Capt. Herbert B. Knowles.
Zeilin, (F), Comdr. Thomas B. Fitzpatrick.

1 XAP:

Perida.

1 APD:

Kane, Lt. Comdr. Freeman D. Miller.

3 DDs:

Dale, Lt. Comdr. Charles W. Aldrich.
Dewey, Lt. Comdr. Joseph P. Canty.
Farragut, Comdr. Henry D. Rozendal.

1 AVD:

Williamson, Lieut. James A. Pridmore.

2 DMs:

Sicard, Lt. Comdr. William J. Richter.
Pruitt, Lt. Comdr. Richard C. Williams, Jr.

(l) *Minesweeper Group.*

2 DMs, Lt. Comdr. Bernhart A. Feutsch:

Chandler, Lt. Comdr. Harry L. Thompson.
Long, (F), Lt. Comdr. Paul F. Heerbrandt.

Tactical Plan

(a) Regimental Landing Group 17 (less Battalion Combat Team 17-1) with Battalion Combat Team 32-2 attached was to land on

D-day at H-hour on Beaches Yellow and Blue in Massacre Bay (see map, p. 112) and attack and destroy the enemy in the Holtz Bay-Chichagof area.

(b) The Composite Battalion, consisting of the 7th Scout Company and the 7th Reconnaissance troop (less one platoon), was to land on D-day in Blind Cove (Beach Scarlet) from the *Narwhal, Nautilus,* and *Kane.*

(c) Battalion Combat Team 17-1 was to await orders afloat off Holtz Bay, ready to land at Beach Scarlet, Massacre Bay, or Sarana Bay, depending upon developments.

(d) One platoon of the 7th Reconnaissance Troop was to land on D-day at Alexai Point (Beach Rainbow).

(e) Support was to be provided by naval gunfire and ground force artillery, as well as by Army and Navy planes. Long-range search by naval aircraft was to take place twice a day. A striking force composed of one-third of available Army heavy and medium bombers was to be held in readiness to destroy all enemy shipping discovered by the search planes. Air liaison parties were assigned to each combat team to transmit requests for support to the attack force commander (Admiral Rockwell). Spotting for naval gunfire would be carried out by battleship or cruiser planes.

(f) Antisubmarine patrol was to be conducted by PBYs based on a tender in Massacre Bay or Sarana Bay.

(g) Reinforcements were to be held at Adak pending developments. A total of approximately 11,000 troops was to be used in the assault, 8000 of them in the main effort at Massacre Bay.

The Approach

The attack force was originally scheduled to leave Cold Bay on 3 May, but bad weather postponed sailing for a day. D-day was then designated as 8 May by Admiral Kinkaid. On the afternoon of the 7th, it appeared likely that surf conditions would be unfavorable on the 8th. D-day was accordingly put off another 24 hours. The *Idaho, Nevada,* and screen were detached at 1800 on the 7th to proceed on westerly courses until in position to support the light cruisers of the Southern Covering Group, now operating to the west of Attu.

Weather continued so inclement that D-day was postponed to the 11th. Simultaneously it was learned that an important enemy convoy, protected by a strong naval force, was probably approaching the Aleutians from the west. Consequently Capt. Buchanan was ordered to take the transports and cargo vessels of the task force and proceed with six destroyers on an easterly course, while the *Pennsylvania* and two destroyers rendezvoused with the *Idaho* group. The battleships made contact with the Southern Covering Group and searched for the enemy throughout the 9th and 10th, but nothing was found. At 1800 on the 10th the battleships rendezvoused with the transports again in a dense fog, while the light cruiser group continued its patrol.

As a glance at a map will show, the assault plan involved widely separated landings. The 7th Scout Company was to land from the submarines on Beach Scarlet at 0300, followed by the 7th Reconnaissance Troop from the *Kane.* Battalion Combat Team 17-1 was to lie off Holtz Bay in the *Bell,* awaiting developments. The other three combat teams were to land in Massacre Bay at 0740. The two areas were separated by about 30 miles, and it was necessary to divide the task force into two groups for the approach. This entailed considerable shifting of units, and was carried out with great difficulty in the all-pervading fog. During these maneuvers the *Sicard* and *MacDonough* collided, with the result that the services of these vessels were lost. The *Sicard* was to have been boat control ship in the Holtz Bay area.

Unavoidable delays necessitated the postponement of H-hour to 0940, and finally to 1040. Had it not been for SG radar equipment, any formation of approach divisions would have been impossible, according to Capt. Corn, commanding officer of the *Pennsylvania*. "The SG radar," he added, "is essential for combatant ships operating in the Aleutian area. The SG radar repeater (PPI) installed on the navigation bridge was invaluable."

At length the two sections of the force felt their way southward in the fog. The Northern Group consisted of the *Pennsylvania, Idaho, Bell, Williamson, Meade, Phelps, Edwards,* and *Farragut.* The *Kane* was not located in time to accompany this formation as planned. The Southern Group was composed of the *Nevada, Zeilin, Heywood, Harris, Perida, Long, Ammen, Hull, Dewey, Dale, Abner Read, Pruitt, Chandler, Elliot,* and *Casco.* The tug *Ute* was also attached to the task force, but her services were lost because of absence of radar for station keeping and lack of suitable communication equipment.

Northern Landings

The approach was uneventful, but arrival off Attu took place in dense fog, contrary to a weather forecast promising clear skies. At 0309 the *Narwhal* disembarked her detachment of the 7th Scout Company, and a few minutes later cleared the beach and returned. At 0510 the *Nautilus* reported that she also had safely landed her part of the 7th Scout Company at Beach Scarlet. The *Kane,* however, which was scheduled to follow with the Reconnaissance Troop, was unable to locate the beach and had to be supplied distance and bearing by the *Pennsylvania's* radar.

At 0927 the *Phelps,* which was acting as northern control vessel in the absence of the *Sicard,* led in eight landing craft with Aleut scouts to determine the feasibility of a landing on Beach Red. *Nassau* planes bombed the Holtz Bay area for half an hour. Later a scout boat reconnoitered Beach Red and reported to the *Bell* at 1205 that beach and surf conditions favored a landing. However, the Landing Force Commander (Maj. Gen. Brown) had directed Combat Team 17-1 to land either at Beach Red or

Beach Scarlet, depending on advices from the scouts who had now been landed at both beaches. No reports had been received, so there was some delay in reaching a decision. Meanwhile the Southern Group off Massacre Bay had asked and received permission to delay its landings because of zero visibility.

The *Kane* had finally landed the Reconnaissance Troop at Beach Scarlet after the Scouts had looked it over and gone on. At 1349 Air reported that the Scouts had reached the pass south of Beach Scarlet. Supplies were dropped to them there an hour later. They sent information that the pass beyond the crest was not feasible for motor vehicles. At 1540 Air reported that the Scouts were completely exhausted and had not moved for three hours, although enemy opposition had apparently not developed.

The hour finally selected for the main northern landing was 1450 and the place Beach Red. A few boats from the *Bell* had already followed the scout boat in, and now the remainder of Combat Team 17-1 went ashore. The *Phelps* had been patrolling around the point of departure since she had led the Aleut scouts in, but she returned to the transport area at 1250 with six empty boats. At this time the *Bell's* signal light was visible only at less than 600 yards. The *Phelps* started back toward the shore with 29 boats at 1410. An hour and a half later she led in six more. Between 1739 and 1754 she searched for empty boats lost in the fog and collected 26 of them, returning them to the transport area by 1903. The remainder of the night was spent in leading other waves to the beach.

Because of the atrocious visibility conditions, no direct gunfire support of these landings was possible for fear of hitting boats and troops. The *Pennsylvania* and *Idaho,* however, began a bombardment of the Chichagof area at 151 to neutralize enemy batteries. Radar control was used, and fire was maintained for an hour.

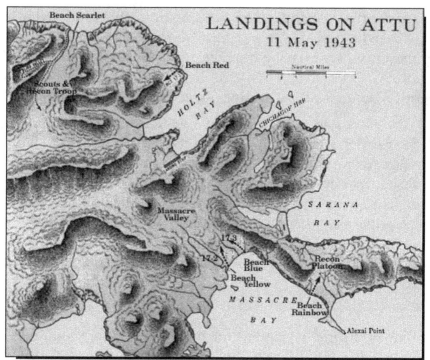

Map 8: Landings on Attu -- 11 May 1943

Southern Landings

The main landings at Massacre Bay proved difficult in the extreme. There were many vaguely charted foul areas which were only partially defined by incomplete information collected in 1934.

The charts showed a track through the bay and stated that no soundings of less than nine fathoms had been discovered. The duties of the control vessel *Pruitt* were further complicated by the faulty visibility. Having no SG radar, the *Pruitt* had to be conned in by the *Dewey*.

As originally scheduled, the first wave was to be preceded by long-range battleship bombardment. Thereafter two destroyers were to enter the bay at either end of the track charted nine years earlier by the *Quail*, close the beaches to give gunfire support, and retire at the opposite end of the track. If visibility was low, which it definitely was, there was danger of collision between the destroyers. This danger was removed, however, by bad weather which forced a cancellation of this portion of the plan.

The Pennsylvania bombards Attu during landing operations of 11 May 1943

At 0815 the transports topped in the transport area. The *Pruitt* closed the *Zeilin* to within 300 yards, but visual communication was often impossible. Boats were lowered, while the *Pruitt* stood off and awaited the formation of waves. At 1020 the *Harris* boat group commander reported. The *Zeilin* group was then mustered and accounted for, except for 6 LCPs which were lost in the fog. They finally rejoined at 1355. H-hour was then scheduled for 1530.

At 1410 the *Pruitt* got underway and headed for the point of departure at 6.5 knots. The fog made it difficult to keep the boat waves in sight, and one of them was soon lost, despite the sounding of "Charlie" on the *Pruitt's* whistle every minute. The group commander was sent back to round the waves up, and the formation lay to from 1422 to 1449 while this was being accomplished. At 1515, on word from the *Dewey*, which was navigating by SG radar, the *Pruitt* started deploying the boats in attack formation. Shortly thereafter four LCMs were dispatched to Beaches Blue and Yellow to fire rockets and return. At 1520 the *Pruitt* reached the point of departure, stopped, and planted a buoy. Visibility had not improved. No land was in sight.

The Pruitt guides landing boats to the beach at Massacre Bay, 11 May 1943

The first wave of 12 LCPs was sent off for Beaches Yellow and Blue on course 320° T., the heading which the ship was maintaining at anchor with the engines. Two reserve boats followed the first wave in, and two LCPs went to Beach Rainbow with one platoon of the Reconnaissance Troop. At 1530 the second wave of 13 LCPs was dispatched to the main landing places. A few minutes later the following message was received from the first wave: "Hit brick wall, what do?" It was thought that the wave had run into the foul area to the east of the objective, so it was instructed to turn left, which proved to be correct.

At 1550 the third wave of ten LCPs went in. Thereupon the *Pruitt* requested Admiral Rockwell's permission to advance within sight of the beach in order to overcome the persistent tendency of coxswains to steer off course to the right. Lacking SG radar, the *Pruitt* had been prevented by the fog from tracking the boats in more than 300-400 yards and had been unable to coach the wave commander by reference to prominent landmarks.

The request was granted. At 1606 the beach was sighted, and, with typical Aleutian fickleness, visibility suddenly lifted to 1,500 yards. Other waves were then dispatched. At 1620 word was received that the first two waves had landed without resistance. Soon radio communications with the beachmaster were established. By 1640 all the remaining waves had landed. The *Pruitt* waited until 1732, when the empty boats had closed her and been accounted for, and then returned to the transport area with the assistance of coaching by the *Dewey*.

The task force commander was informed that six waves had landed at Beach Blue, three at Beach Yellow, and one at Beach Rainbow. No opposition had been encountered anywhere, nor did the troops on Beach Yellow meet the enemy while driving about 2,000 yards inland before 1800. The only casualties were those caused by an accident during the second boat trip from the *Heywood*. In the murk, Boat No. 13 hit a submerged object. The bow man thought it had touched shore and released the ramp safety hooks in preparation for landing. The brake on the winch then tripped accidentally, dropping the ramp. The boat was going full speed, and despite all effort of personnel it filled with water and sank, drowning four soldiers.

By 2000 the troops at Beach Red had advanced 1,500 yards, noting some firing which was presumed to come from our own forces. By 2130, 1,100 troops were ashore at this beach, 2,000 at Yellow and Blue, and 400 at Scarlet.

During the first trip to the southern beaches, considerable difficulty was experienced because of the necessity of interchanging landing craft between transports so that complete combat teams could be landed. During the second trip the fog was so dense that each ship was directed to use its own boats. This trip landed about 2255. Shortly thereafter Commander Landing Force set up his command post on Beach Yellow.

Except for the brief bombing in the morning by *Nassau* planes, the weather permitted no effective air support. Army planes remained overhead, however, and were occasionally able to make valuable reports on progress of units such as the Scout Company at Beach Scarlet and drop supplies to them.

Apparently the enemy did not discover our landings until about 1510, and complete tactical surprise was achieved. All in all, progress was most encouraging. It had been estimated that one full day would be required for the capture of the airfield, and it still seemed that this length of time would not be much exceeded.

Events of 12 May

The following morning saw little improvement in the weather, although at 0420 visibility in Massacre Bay had temporarily increased so that the transports were able to see each other for the first time since their arrival.

Upon request of Shore Fire Control Party No. 3, the *Pennsylvania* delivered an hour's neutralization fire against enemy targets in the West Arm of Holtz Bay. Communications were good, and the bombardment, in which both 14-inch HC and 5-inch 38 caliber AA common were used, was reported most effective.

At 1158 the air liaison officer reported to Admiral Rockwell that the Holtz Bay area was sufficiently open to permit air bombing and strafing. A flight from the *Nassau* was sent in to operate against that sector with 100-pound demolition bombs and machine guns. Heavy antiaircraft fire was encountered. Shortly thereafter, Army bombers were able to carry out an attack against targets to the rear of the East Arm. The air coordinator reported heavy antiaircraft fire from two targets in the beach area. At 1400 the *Idaho* fired 48 rounds of 14-inch HC at an average range of 18,000 yards to try to neutralize these targets.

Beach Red suffered from intermittent enemy artillery fire throughout the day. The *Phelps* was ordered to deal with targets in the Chichagof area which were suspected of being responsible for this annoyance, while at 1537 the *Idaho* fired 200 rounds of 14-inch into the West Arm to support attacks by Combat Team 17-1, which had finally run into strong enemy resistance. Though the day's gunfire support of the northern landings was reported as being well-delivered and effective, it did not succeed in actually destroying the artillery targets.

The *Bell* continued unloading off Beach Red all day, a tedious process, because rocks permitted only one or two boats to go ashore at a time. As a result, the ship was thoroughly exposed to submarine attack, but none eventuated.

In the southern area, meanwhile, the *Nevada* and *Abner Read* had supported our troops with heavy gunfire several times during the day, paying particular attention to the Massacre Bay-Holtz Bay passes. Shore fire control was employed. The *Nevada* silenced an enemy mountain battery, and results were believed to have been generally excellent.

Combat Team 32-2 from the *Perida* began to go ashore during the morning, the first boats reaching the beach about 1140, after the fog had again closed in. Three hours later, weather conditions permitted the transports to move in. The *Long, Elliot,* and *Chandler* swept the channel into Massacre Bay, and the *Ute* led the *Zeilin* in by about 500 yards. Immediately upon anchoring, continuous unloading was begun, as well as evacuation of casualties from the beach. Slight interruptions began to occur at 1700, when berths were shifted as a result of a survey of the bay which was being completed by the *Ute, Pruitt,* and *Hydrographer* (Comdr. William M. Scaife, Jr.). During one of the moves, the *Perida* struck a pinnacle, ruptured holds No. 1 and No. 2. The *Hydrographer* was ordered to sound a course from the *Perida* to the beach, while the *Ute* stood by to assist the stricken vessel. The *Perida* reported that it would be necessary to run her bow ashore to prevent further flooding and requested the location of a suitable shoal. She was told to use Beach

Yellow. At 2010, with five feet of water in No. 1 hold and seven feet in No. 2, she was run on the west end of Beach Yellow. The *Ute* stood by to keep the damaged ship's stern to seaward and to assist in salvage operations. Other ships were directed to send one LCM(3) apiece to help discharge the flooded holds. The *Hydrographer* was then ordered to complete a survey of the bay, placing navigational aids which consisted in the main of empty gasoline drums supplied by the *Zeilin*.

The situation ashore was not so favorable as had been hoped at the end of the previous day. The troops were finding the going very difficult, and the number available for combat was greatly diminished by an unforeseen circumstance. It was found almost impossible to operate trucks and tractors in the Attu mud, with the result that many soldiers had to be assigned to labor duties. At the urgent request of Commander Landing Force, Admiral Rockwell directed the *Chirikof* and the *Grant* (Capt. Charles L. Hutton), which were remaining within ten hours steaming distance, to approach and land their reserve troops, although he felt some hesitation in issuing this order until the transports already in Massacre Bay had been unloaded.

Shortly thereafter there was considerable excitement in the Holtz Bay area when the *Pennsylvania,* which was moving offshore, saw a torpedo approaching. Successful evasive action was taken.

At midnight the first casualty report reached the task force commander. Forty-four officers and men had been killed so far. It also became know at this time that progress inland had ceased in the Massacre Bay sector, both battalion combat teams being pinned down by machine-gun fire. Commander Landing Force expressed the opinion that results would be best and most quickly achieved by commitment of another battalion from those aboard the *Chirikof* and *Grant.*

As on the previous day, visibility limited the amount of air support which could be offered. Several missions, however, were accomplished by both carrier and Army planes under conditions of great danger. The *Casco* moved into Massacre Bay, and six PBYs and four battleship OS2Us based on her. When the latter were not spotting gunfire or flying antisubmarine patrols, they dropped depth bombs with instantaneous fuzes on isolated Japanese positions.

The control of all air support remained in the hands of Admiral Rockwell until 16 May, when it was turned over to Commander Landing Force. During the period of the attack, the *Nassau* cruised off Holtz Bay and northeast of Attu. Because of the necessity of taking advantage of brief breaks in the weather, she rarely operated more than 40 miles from the target area. Sometimes she ventured within ten miles of Holtz Bay. When she steamed independently of the task force, antisubmarine coverage was provided by PBYs and destroyers.

Events of 13 May

The weather was still adverse on the 13th. The fog made air support and naval gunfire not only difficult but at times impossible. Beach Red had been shelled intermittently by the enemy during the night, and it was still under fire in the morning, preventing the unloading of boats. The artillery of Battalion Combat Team 17-1 was receiving considerable attention from Japanese guns on the tongue of Holtz Bay and apparently could not be got into action to neutralize the enemy batteries. Erroneous reports were received of an enemy landing behind our lines, either at Beach Red or in the West Arm of Holtz Bay. In some accounts the situation was alleged to be desperate, and immediate reinforcements were urgently requested. Commander Landing Force, whose headquarters, as has been sated, were in the southern landing area on Beach Yellow, thereupon delegated an officer to take direct command at Beach Red, and no further alarming reports were received.

At 1200 the transports *Grant* and *Chirikof,* escorted by the gunboat *Charleston,* arrived at Massacre Bay with their reinforcements. At this juncture enemy resistance in the Holtz Bay was so determined that the *Chirikof* was directed to proceed to the northern landings area and land her battalion combat team at Beach Red. Fog delayed arrival at that point until 1730, when boats from the *Bell* were immediately employed in effecting landings. Because of the restricted approaches already mentioned, these were not completed until 1030 the next morning. The *Grant,* however, unloaded at Massacre Bay by 2100.

Unloading supplies on Attu, 13 May 1943

The *Nevada* bombarded targets in the southern landing area four times during the day. Progress in this sector was negligible, however, and at about 2300 Commander Landing Force recommended landing further reinforcements which were still at Adak. Commander transports reported at 2400 that the APAs were 55 per cent unloaded, the *Perida* 14 percent, and that the *Hydrographer* was making progress in buoying a safe entrance channel to Massacre Bay and expected to complete the work in 24 hours.

In the northern landing area, the *Idaho* and *Phelps* executed minor fire support missions whenever the weather let up. From 1713 to 1800, planes from the *Nassau* armed with 100-pound demolition bombs made five to seven runs apiece, strafing and bombing enemy barges in Holtz Bay which were reported to be lobbing shells into our lines. Japanese machine guns were also silenced, enabling our troops to move to new positions and set up their artillery. Hitherto the guns with Combat Team 17-1 had been silent because of enemy shelling. It was fortunate that they were able to open up at last, because at 1818 Admiral Rockwell informed Commander Landing Force that the ships were running low on ammunition.

Events of 14 May

Next morning visibility was still low, and little progress was made ashore. In the afternoon, however, the Army units in the West Arm, supported by Combat Team 32-3 (newly landed from the *Chirikof*), assaulted Japanese positions. Air cooperation could not be rendered because of the weather, but the artillery at Beach Red gave a good account of itself. Thereafter the *Pennsylvania* fired almost continuously for two hours and a half to support a coordinated attack which jumped off at 1600. Bad visibility required that the ship's position be established by radar. Both main and secondary batteries were used, air bursts being employed for the 5-inch firing.

The troops managed to advance only 500 yards, but Admiral Rockwell considered this fire support the most successful of the entire operation because it was closely integrated with the ground effort. Enemy positions were well dug in and gun positions well defiladed, but neutralization was accomplished.

The Army reported that the battle in the Holtz Bay area was in a critical state, but that if naval gunfire could be kept up, our troops could forge ahead. Consequently, some time after the flagship had ceased firing, the *Phelps* was sent in to back up the advance and fired 677 round of 5-inch. Spotters stated that fire was "excellently done."

Admiral Rockwell informed Commander Landing Force that Admiral Kinkaid felt the need of prompt action to secure Attu and pointed out that the naval task force must be ready to meet strong Japanese naval forces possibly assembling in the North Pacific. In connection with his request for reinforcements from Adak, General Brown was asked to furnish an estimate of the situation.

Meanwhile Commander Landing Force had reported that little progress was being made in dealing with the entrenched positions in the mouths of the passes between Massacre and Holtz Bays and said that he intended to resume the attack in the morning. Later, in estimating the situation as requested, he ascribed the slow progress to difficult terrain, greater enemy forces than had been expected, as evidenced by captured documents, and lack of sufficient troops to accomplish his mission.

Carrier air activities during the day were limited to two flights of four Wildcats, dispatched in response to urgent requests from troops. The weather was so severe that four planes and three pilots were lost.

One flight each of Army B-25s and B-24s managed to reach the area. The B-25s were unable to drop, but the B-24s "made a daring flight" and bombed targets in the East Arm of Holtz Bay. Another B-24, in an effort to get provisions to forward elements, crashed in a mountain pass.

By the early afternoon of the 14th, the *Nevada* and *Idaho* had expended all their 14-inch HC ammunition. Because of this and the increasing submarine threat, the force commander ordered them to proceed northward with their screen and await orders. At the end of the day, the unloading situation was as follows: *Heywood*, 100 per cent; *Zeilin*, 90 per cent; *Harris*, 72 per cent; *Grant*, 50 percent; *Perida*, 30 per cent.

Events of 15 May

At 0525 on 15 May, the *Bell* in Holtz Bay reported that she was 70 percent unloaded, while the *Chirikof* had discharged 10

---

per cent of her cargo. Intermittent shelling of Beach Red by the enemy was still slowing the landing of supplies.

Attacks scheduled for the morning were delayed by the usual poor visibility. Commander Landing Force again recommended to Admiral Rockwell that reinforcements be sent from Adak, saying that they might make all the difference between the success and failure of the operation. In order that all concerned might fully understand the situation, he requested a conference with Admiral Rockwell, Admiral Kinkaid, and General DeWitt.

At 1140 four torpedoes passed on either side of the *Bell* and not far from the *Pennsylvania*. Attempts to destroy the submarine were unsuccessful. The *Bell* was temporarily withdrawn from the area to avoid further attacks.

A fuller estimate of the situation was received from General Brown and forwarded with comments to Admiral Kinkaid by Admiral Rockwell. The task force commander recommended that the requested reinforcements be sent, as well as tugs, barges, and other smaller craft to promote local mobility, that maximum air support be afforded, but the naval gunfire support be withdrawn. He further stated that the landing phase of the operation would be completed with the withdrawal of the APAs, and that the *Pennsylvania* and *Nassau* should sail in company with them.

At 1410 General Brown came aboard the *Pennsylvania* and urgently reiterated his requests for reinforcements, saying that all available forces were now committed, and that without additional strength it would not be possible to take Attu. Admiral Rockwell reported the results of this conference to Admiral Kinkaid and said that the *Bell* had been ordered to return to Beach Red with the hope of completing unloading next day so that she and the *Harris* and *Zeilin* might be sent to Adak to load troops if Admiral Kinkaid so directed.

At the conference captured Japanese documents were produced which indicated that the size of the enemy force was between 2,000 and 2,500 men.

The troops in the southern landing area made little headway during the day, but the northern forces, which had at length been joined by the troops from Beach Scarlet, had advanced two-thirds of the way across the valley of the West Arm of Holtz Bay. At 1700, however, Beach Red was still undergoing artillery fire from the East Arm.

Weather prevented carrier operations, but an Army B-24 managed to drop urgently needed supplies to the provisional battalion (the troops from Beach Scarlet). A flight of P-38s arrived during the late afternoon simultaneously with a break in the weather, and delivered an effective attack on Japanese forces opposing our northern troops, including the antiaircraft artillery in the East Arm.

Events of 16 May

On the morning of the 16th the northern landing force attacked under air cover supplied by the *Nassau*. Three sections of planes, under extremely difficult weather conditions, bombed and strafed Holtz Bay targets. Two planes and two pilots were lost. Upon learning that continuing air support was necessary if the ground troops were to progress, the *Nassau* launched another attack at 1024. The *Abner Read* also supported the northern attack at 1800, firing 138 rounds. Three flights of Army bombers and two flights of P038s reached the area during the day, but weather prevented the bombers from making their drops. The P-38s came in under the overcast and bombed and strafed targets in Holtz Bay and the Chichagof area. A B-24 brining in supplies to advance troops dropped them on Beach Red rather than carry them back to base.

Admiral Rockwell was informed during the morning that one battalion of the 4th Infantry would leave Adak on the 17th in the *St. Mihiel* to arrive early the next evening. At 1910 the attack force commander directed Capt. Knowles in the *Heywood* to assume local naval control, and the *Pennsylvania* in company with the *Abner Read, Ammen,* and *Pruitt,* and the *Nassau* with the *Aylwin* and *Meade,* withdrew to the northward. Air-ground control passed to Commander Landing Force at 2000. At 2130 the *Zeilin, Harris,* and *Bell,* having discharged all their cargo, departed for Adak with their screen.

At 2210 Maj. Gen. Eugene Landrum reported to Admiral Rockwell that he had assumed command of the landing force by order of Admiral Kinkaid.

Events of 17-18 May

Throughout the next day, the *Pennsylvania* and *Nassau* operated to the north of Attu. Weather prevented the use of carrier aircraft. At the island itself, the *Phelps* neutralized targets in Holtz Bay during the morning. Later she destroyed some barges in Chichagof Harbor. The northern landing force advanced, and by 2100 General Landrum reported that the enemy had been driven from the East Arm of Holtz Bay, adding that casualties with frostbitten feet were outnumbering other types by two to one. Unloading of the *Perida* and *Chirkof* continued at Massacre Bay.

The following day General Landrum informed Admiral Kinkaid of his future plans. He requested two rifle companies, a firing battery, and the headquarters unit of the 32d Infantry at Adak, as well as freighters containing 105-mm. ammunition, which was running short. Further he asked that one attack transport be retained at Adak to move up additional reinforcements.

Later in the morning the rest of the Holtz Bay area was cleared of the enemy, and contact was reported between the southern and northern sections of the landing force. Consequently, at 1633, Admiral Kinkaid informed Admiral Rockwell that when the *St. Mihiel* arrived at Massacre Bay the landing force would become Attu Occupation Force. Thereafter Admiral Rockwell was to retire to Adak, leaving the SOPA in the *Heywood* (Capt. Knowles) in naval control. Admiral Rockwell told General Landrum that the *Aylwin, Meade,* and *Phelps* (the first-named when she had completed her duty with the *Nassau's* screen) would be available for gunfire support. He also notified Admiral Kinkaid of his intention toepart at 0600 on the 19th. At 2218 the landing phase of the operation was completed.

Attack on *Phelps* and *Charleston,* 22 May

The clearing out of the remaining Japanese forces on Attu was facilitated between 19 and 21 May by minor bombardment missions performed by the destroyer *Meade* and the 6-inch gunboat *Charleston* (Comdr. Gordon B. Sherwood). On the afternoon of the 22d the *Charleston* and the destroyer *Phelps* were patrolling off the entrance to Holtz Bay when 12 to 18 Mitsubishi Type 01 twin-engine heavy bombers appeared out of the fog and delivered a torpedo and strafing attack. Six planes concentrated on the *Charleston* and the rest on the *Phelps.* No torpedoes found their mark.

One passed 50 yards ahead of the *Charleston,* one paralleled the ship 25 yards to port, and two passed 50 and 100 yards astern respectively. The *Charleston* was struck by 17 bullets, the *Phelps* by eight. One plane crashed about three miles away, under fire from both ships. One torpedo was exploded by gunfire as it was dropping.

The next day another air attack on Attu by 126 Bettys was intercepted over Cape Wrangell by six P-38s, and the Japanese planes were forced to jettison their bombs. Five hostile aircraft were shot down. We lost two P-38s and one pilot.

On the morning of the 24th the *Phelps* conducted a final bombardment, expending 426 rounds of 5-inch 38 caliber antiaircraft common. At 1155 the destroyer departed for Adak accompanied by the *Meade.* The *Charleston* continued her support work on the 25th and 26th. On those days and on the 22d she expended a total of 951 rounds of 6-inch 47 ammunition.

Airfields on Attu and Shemya Established

It was early discovered that the site of the incomplete enemy airfield on Attu was not well chosen. Consequently it was abandoned and two new fighter strips were constructed at Alexai point. The first of these was operational by 9 June.

After preliminary reconnaissance, the island of Shemya was occupied on 30 May by Army troops under command of Brig. Gen. Copeland. The landing was made without opposition, and Army engineers immediately began construction of a bomber runway which was ultimately to be 10,000 feet long. By 21 June 3,000 feet were complete, and fighters could operate.

Note on the Effect of Naval Gunfire; Air Operations

In the attack on Attu it was again demonstrated that naval gunfire was primarily useful for neutralization, not for destruction. Not only did the guns of our task force perform the former function effectively, furthering the advance of the troops whenever the latter were in a position to take immediate advantage of its results, but their fire had a stimulating effect on the morale of our men. Conversely, naval gunfire had a "tremendous harassing effect on the enemy," according to observers. Captured diaries referred constantly to the casualties it caused and to the shattering of the nerves of the defenders. Many Japanese, under fire for the first time, "seemed surprised at the intensity and effectiveness of our fire."

When supported from the air and by naval gunfire, our troops were able in most instances to advance with only minor casualties; but when such support was limited by conditions of poor visibility, the men were pinned to the ground by enemy fire and suffered severely. The entire operation was thus modified, like every phase of the Aleutians Campaign, by the variability of weather conditions and the prevalence of fog and winds.

The foul weather, and the nature of the terrain and of the Japanese defenses, required the support force to use large quantities of ammunition to achieve neutralization of enemy positions, a fact which might have handicapped our vessels had effective Japanese naval opposition developed.

The air forces, both Army and Navy, accomplished many missions under the most hazardous conditions and did everything they could to support the ground troops. Weather, however, hampered aerial activity on every day of the operation proper. At no time was it possible for the *Nassau* to launch and all-out air attack. Very rarely could more than four planes operate efficiently against an enemy position. It was not considered advisable to risk having a total of more than eight planes in the air at once lest a shift of weather prevent recovery.

Because of insufficient wind over the flight deck, the *Nassau* had to catapult every one of the 179 planes launched. The loss of five pilots was considered low, in view of the lack of training, the nature of the operation, and, again, the weather.

Note on Rations Supplied by Transports

During the assault, the transports regularly supplied hot food for the troops and beach parties. The part played by the *Harris* is illustrative:

During the landing operations, hot food for approximately 1,200 Army personnel was sent to the beach twice daily. Food consisted of hot coffee, cocoa, stew, chili and beans, and corned beef mulligan. Tags marked "FOR FRONT LINE TROOPS ONLY" were attached to food containers, and reports were received aboard ships that the food arrived satisfactorily at the front lines. In addition, 60 rations were sent to the *Harris* beach party, and after the first day, at the request of the beachmaster, this was increased to 300 rations to include Army personnel working with the beach party. Supplying boat crews with hot food, coffee, and box lunches presents no special problem. Ship's cooks, bakers, and stewards' mates were stationed on the upper decks at all times ready to lower food into the boats which were being loaded alongside. Cigarettes, cigars, matches, and candy were given to the beach party and boat crews daily, and an additional 5,000 packages of cigarettes and matches and several thousand candy bars were sent to front line troops.

Chapter 12: Softening Up Kiska

In preparation for the next move in the Aleutian Campaign, the occupation of Kiska, both surface bombardment and bombing played important parts. The 11th Air Force did heroic work under difficult conditions. From 24 May to 15 August Kiska received a total of 600 tons of explosives as a result of surface bombardment, while 1,310 tons were dropped from the air. In addition to bombing, much strafing was done. Total sorties were 1,581. Captured diaries bear eloquent witness to the physical and moral effects of the continuous raids.

Obviously the figures for bombing (as, indeed, the figures for bombardment) are in no way comparable to those reached in later campaigns against enemy-held islands farther south. It must be remembered, however, that the air forces involved in the Aleutians Campaign were never large, and that weather conditions offered impediments to air activity which were matched in no other theater of war. The obstacles overcome by our airmen in conducting their ceaseless attacks would have been considered insuperable at the outset of the war.

It is now known that on 8 June Rear Admiral Akiyama issued orders for the abandonment of Kiska. There was no way in which our high command could learn of this enemy decision, so plans for the seizure of the island went forward rapidly during the month of June, while the 11th Air Force dropped 262 tons of bombs with the loss of but two planes. (The bomb weight was held to this low figure by execrable weather.)

During the major part of the period from 24 May to 15 August, a task group of cruisers and destroyers was on station north or south of Kiska. Frequently task groups operated both north and south of the island. From 8 June a destroyer blockade was maintained continuously, with the exception of 23 and 24 July, when a submarine was on patrol to the west.

Bombardment of 6 July

With the coming of July our major surface forces began to take an active hand in the softening up process. On the afternoon of 6 July Kiska was subjected to a 22-minute bombardment by Task Group George (Rear Admiral Robert C. Giffen). Ships involved were the *Wichita* (F) (Capt. John J. Mahoney), *Louisville* (now commanded by Capt. Alexander S. Wotherspoon), *San Francisco* (Capt. Albert F. France), *Santa Fe* (Capt. Russell S. Berkey), *Hughes* (Lt. Comdr. Herbert H. Marable), *Lansdowne* (Lt. Comdr. Francis J. Foley), *Morris* (Lt. Comdr. Edward S. Burns), and *Mustin* (Lt. Comdr. Earl T. Schreiber). The two last-named destroyers took no part in the bombardment proper, having been assigned as anti-submarine screen for the main force.

No enemy opposition was encountered, except sporadic and ineffective antiaircraft fire directed against spotting planes. Target areas were thought to have been thoroughly covered, although observation of results was not generally possible because of overcast and other factors. Particular attention was devoted to coast defense batteries believed to be located on North Head and Little Kiska, antiaircraft batteries at Gertrude Cove and South Head, and the Main Camp area.

Under the fairly good visibility conditions, the 6-inch coast defense guns on Little Kiska were regarded as the primary threat to our vessels. The *Santa Fe*, with her superior volume of fire, was therefore assigned to lead the cruiser column, smothering this target during the first few minutes, after which she was to swing around to take position astern of the other cruisers. It was, of course, impossible to tell whether this procedure was responsible for the fact that the enemy batteries did not fire. Planes from Amchitka were bombing Kiska during the bombardment, and this may have preoccupied Japanese personnel to an extent which prevented opening fire. It is more likely, however, that the enemy did not wish to disclose his positions.

View from the Wichita during pre-invasion bombardment of Kiska, 6 July 1943

Not long after firing ceased, the fog closed in. Had the bombardment been delayed an hour, no air spot would have been possible.

In the course of the shelling, the following ammunition was expended: 312 round 8-inch 55-caliber, 256 6-inch 47 caliber, 1,158 5-inch 38 caliber, 92 5-inch 25 caliber (about 100 tons).

During the rest of July, Kiska was bombarded a number of times by destroyers of our blockade force, as follows:

 9 July — *Aylwin,* 100 rounds
10 July — *Monaghan,* 100 rounds
14 July — *Monaghan,* 100 rounds
15 July — *Monaghan,* 100 rounds
20 July — *Aylwin* and *Monaghan,* 200 rounds
30 July — *Farragut* and *Hull,* 200 rounds

Little return fire was received and there was no conclusive evidence of important damage to the enemy. "However, the purpose, that of harassing the enemy, was accomplished," according to CINCPAC.

Bombardment of 22 July

On 22 July Kiska was subjected to a heavy combined air and surface bombardment. Two task groups were involved. These were organized as follows:

Task Group George, Rear Admiral Robert C. Giffen.

Three heavy cruisers:

Louisville, Capt. Alexander S. Wotherspoon.
San Francisco, Capt. Albert F. France.
Wichita, (F), Capt. John J. Mahoney.

One light cruiser:

Santa Fe, Russell S. Berkey.

Five destroyers:

Aylwin, Lt. Comdr. Ray E. Malpass.
Bache, Comdr. Frank M. Adamson.
Hughes, Lt. Comdr. Herbert H. Marable.
Morris, Lt. Comdr. Edward S. Burns.
Mustin, Lt. Comdr. Earl T. Schreiber.

Task Group Gilbert, Rear Admiral Robert M. Griffin.

Two battleships:

Mississippi, Capt. Lunsford L. Hunter.
New Mexico, (F) Capt. Oliver L. Downes.

One heavy cruiser:

Portland, Capt. Arthur D. Burhans.

Four destroyers:

Abner Read, Comdr. Thomas Burrowes (Commander Screen).
Farragut, (F, Comdr. George R. Cooper, ComDesDiv Two), Lt. Comdr. Edward F. Ferguson.
Monaghan, Lt. Comdr. Peter H. Horn.
Perry, Lt. Comdr. Bernhart A. Fuetsch.

The battleship group approached from the north and the cruiser group from the south. Army planes bombed the island during the approach. Task Group George fired on the main camp and Little Kiska for 21 minutes, while Task Group Gilbert fired for 18 minutes on batteries at North Head, South Head, Sunrise Hill, and the submarine base.

Enemy resistance was negligible, and the bombardment proceeded exactly according to plan. Indirect fire was used throughout, though the weather was exceptionally clear. Gunnery performance was excellent. The only disquieting occurrences were "frequent reports of submarines caused by at least two porpoises and three whales sighted in the area between the bombardment track and Kiska Harbor."

Aerial photos indicated that all targets had been well covered. The Commanding General 116th Air Force flew past Kiska in the afternoon and reported that the entire area from north of Salmon Lagoon to south of Gertrude Cove was on fire as a result of shells and bombs.

Ammunition expended by the task groups was as follows (about 212 tons):

Caliber	Task Group George	Task Group Gilbert
14-inch HC		123
8-inch HC	345	63
6-inch HC	300	
5-inch 51 caliber HC		272
5-inch 38 caliber AA common	942	615
5-inch 25 caliber AA	132	11
Totals:	1,719	1,084

No enemy batteries fired on Task Group George. Only one battery, composed of four 75-mm., was believed to have directed fire at Task Group Gilbert.

Radar Contacts of 25-26 July

During the last week of July, several radar contacts which were never positively identified were made west of the islands. on 23 July a Catalina on patrol made radar contact at 1224 with seven vessels in latitude 49°50′ N., longitude 170°04′ E., about 200 miles southwest of Attu. This was at first presumed to be Task Group George, but was not. During darkness on 26 July both task groups operating in company, made a radar contact 90 miles southwest of Kiska and took it under fire at ranges of 12,000-20,000 yards. Starshells were used, but the target was never seen, and daylight searches by aircraft and ships failed to reveal anything. Radar officers later suggested that the contacts might have been caused by triple-trip echoes from Amchitka, about 110 miles away, brought about by unusual atmospheric conditions. Using this hypothesis in the case of the *New Mexico*, target course and speed could have been developed by the use of ranges of about 23,000 yards, instead of 223,000 (the distance to Amchitka), which finally gave target course approximately parallel to the American force and speed slightly less.

The heavy ships of Task Group Gilbert alone punished the phantoms with 518 14-inch shells, 485 8-inch, 25 5-inch 38 caliber, and 76 5-inch 25 caliber.

At 0840 on 29 July a Catalina made radar contact with 7 ships about 200 miles northwest of Attu. Contact was maintained until 1045 and then lost. Because of the fog, the vessels could never be identified. Perhaps they were engaged in evacuating Kiska.

Bombardment of 2 August

On the afternoon of 2 August, Task Group Baker (Rear Admiral Wilder D. Baker) and Task Group King (Rear Admiral Howard F. Kingman) carried out a combined bombardment, the former from the south, the latter from the north. The groups were organized as follows:

Task Group Baker

Two heavy cruisers:

Salt Lake City, Capt. Bertram J. Rodgers.
Indianapolis, Capt. Einar R. Johnson.

Three light cruisers:

Richmond, Capt. William A.S. Macklin.
Detroit, Capt. Ellis H. Geiselman.
Raleigh, Capt. Albert T. Srapgue, Jr.

Five destroyers, Capt Wyatt Craig, ComDesRon 14:

Edwards, Lt. Comdr. Paul G. Osler.
Farragut, Lt. Comdr. Edward F. Ferguson.
Frazier, Lt. Comdr. Elliott M. Brown.
Gansevoort, Lt. Comdr. Montgomery L. McCullough, Jr.
Meade, Lt. Comdr. John Munholland.

Task Group King

Two battleships:

Idaho, Capt. Horace D. Clarke.

Tennessee, (F), Capt. Robert S. Haggart.

Four destroyers, Capt. Ruthven E. Libby:

Anderson, Lt. Comdr. John G. Tennent, III.
Aylwin, Lt. Comdr. Ray E. Malpass.
Dale, Lt. Comdr. Charles WS. Aldrich.
Phelps, Lt. Comdr. John E. Edwards

The weather was clear at sea level, with a slight surface haze. The ceiling was about 1,000 feet. The bombardment was coordinated with bombing by 18 Liberators which lasted from 1610 to 1700. Task Group Baker covered targets in the area of Gertrude Cove, Main Camp, the west end of Little Kiska, and the South Head batteries. Task Group King covered North Head and the submarine base. There was no retaliatory fire. Ammunition expended is listed below (about 185 tons):

Caliber	Task Group King	Task Group Baker
14-inch HC	120	
8-inch HC		250
6-inch HC		605
5-inch	931	406
Totals:	1,051	1,261

Bombardments were also conducted during this period by the destroyers of the Kiska blockade, two of which remained continually on station. Ten such bombardments were executed between 2 and 15 August by the *Abner Read, Aylwin, Farragut, Hull, Monaghan,* and *Phelps.* A total of 994 rounds of 5-inch ammunition was expended.

Bombardment of 12 August

On 12 August another pre-dawn bombardment was carried out by Task Group Baker, with the *Phelps* taking the place of the *Farragut*. Firing lasted from 0712 to 0733. Ammunition expended was 85 rounds of 8-inch, 450 of 6-inch, and 1,072 of 5-inch, or about 50 tons. Spotting planes reported target areas well covered, but damage was, as usual, difficult to assess, particularly because of the excellence of the enemy's camouflage. There was no return fire, except small arms and tracer, and possibly a few rounds from a battery on the west side of Jeff Cove. The bombardment was followed by two days of aerial attacks, involving 128 planes which dropped 87 tons of bombs.

Chapter 13: The Invasion of Kiska
15 August 1943

Plans for the Assault

Although the occupation of Kiska was achieved without enemy opposition, it nevertheless was conducted under combat conditions until the landing was well underway.

Considerably larger forces were allotted to the assault on Kiska than had been used at Attu, since the garrison of the former island was known to have been several times as large as Attu's. The landing force consisted of 34,426 troops, 5,300 of whom were Canadian. Ships involved were three battleships, one heavy cruiser, one light cruiser, nineteen destroyers, five attack transports, one attack cargo vessel, ten transports, three cargo vessels, one fast transport, fourteen LSTs, nine LCI(L)s, nineteen LCT(5)s, two light minelayers, three fast minesweepers, two tugs, one harbor tug, and one surveying ship. Potential air strength was 24 heavy bombers, 44 medium bombers, 28 dive bombers, 60 fighters, and 12 patrol bombers. Command of the attack force was vested in Admiral Rockwell, while Maj. Gen. C.H. Corlett was to command the landing force.

Supreme command was again in the hands of Thomas C. Kinkaid, who had been promoted to Vice Admiral.

As soon as success at Attu was assured, plans for the attack on Kiska were placed in work. In this case it was possible for shore party and fire control party personnel with experience at Attu to be sent to California for training exercises. The troops eventually employed consisted of the 17th Infantry, 53d Infantry, 87th Mountain Infantry, 184th Infantry, First Special Service Force, 13th Canadian Infantry Brigade Group, and headquarters troops. The 17th Infantry was to be returned to Adak from Attu, where the 159th would replace it. The 53d Infantry was a composite group organized in Alaska. The 87th Mountain Infantry reported at Fort Ord on 19 June. The 13th Canadian Infantry Brigade assembled on Vancouver Island between 1 and 15 June.

With the exception of the 17th Infantry, most of these units had had no significant amphibious training. The First Special Service Force, however, consisted of about 1,800 men especially trained in commando tactics, rubber boat handling, and parachuting. While the majority of the men involved were to receive preliminary training outside the Alaskan area, experience at Attu had shown that it was essential for troops unfamiliar with the Aleutian terrain to have at least two weeks' training in the area itself.

The plans for the assault proper were approved on 19 July by Admiral Kinkaid. The 87th Mountain Infantry conducted training exercises and San Diego and Fort Ord under the supervision of Admiral Rockwell and General Corlett, while the Commanding General, Amphibious Corps, Pacific Fleet (Maj. Gen. Holland M. Smith, USMC) and his staff conducted the training in the Adak area. On 22 July Admiral Rockwell and General Corlett left San Francisco in the *Grant,* which had been fitted as an advanced command post for the landing force commander. (Admiral Rockwell's flagship, the *Pennsylvania,* which was being refitted as a headquarters ship, was not to be ready until 3 August).

The target date had been set as 15 August, but at a conference of all ranking officers at Adak on 30 July it was decided to delay D-day until the 24th because of the need for further training and regrouping of battalion combat teams. This decision was not acceptable to CINCPAC, so D-day was again designated as 15 August and H-hour as 0630.

Invasion fleet gathers in Adak Harbor for assault on Kiska

It was believed that the main enemy positions had been laid out to meet attack from the south and east. An interesting plan was evolved to capitalize on this concentration of defensive power. Major fire support was to be delivered from the south and east against known Japanese gun positions. Simultaneously one transport group was to make a feint from the south. The actual landings, however, were to be made on the north and west side of the island, facing our major fire support.

The initial landings were to take place on the north side of the central portion of the island, preceded by night landings by the special service force, which was directed to seize high ground to the southward of the beaches. On D plus 1 day new beachheads were to be secured on the west side of the northern part of Kiska. This later operation was to be carried out by transports which had previously conducted the demonstration on the southern side of the island.

Most of the heavier ships which had conducted the bombardments of 22 July and 2 August were to operate to the south and west of Kiska and Attu to cover the landing.

On 13 August both transport groups departed from Adak for Kiska. At 1700 they were followed by the *Pennsylvania, Idaho, Tennessee, Santa Fe,* and their screens.

Execution of the Plan

Early in the morning of the 15th, minesweepers cleared the necessary channels, after which transports took up positions in Transport Area No. 1 (northwest of the waist of the island). Battleships, cruisers, and destroyers executed prearranged fires on targets in the Gertrude Cove, Little Kiska, North Head, Main Camp, and submarine base areas. The five transports which were eventually to constitute the northern group then assembled south of the central portion of the island in order to conduct their demonstration. Five motor torpedo boats arrived in this area at 0750 and went in for reconnaissance. They were camouflaged with wood to give the impression that large landing parties were aboard.

Meanwhile the southern landing ships group had arrived and joined the transports on the north side of the island. The first assault wave, covered by special service troops which were already ashore, landed at 0621. No opposition was encountered. In spite of congestion and unsuitability of some of the beaches, 3,000 men had reached the island by 1200 and had established a beachhead 4,500 yards long. By 1600 a total of 6,500 troops had been landed.

The lack of contact with enemy forces was unexpected, but it was not wholly surprising. Intelligence had suggested that the Japanese might withdraw to prepared positions on the high ground back of the beaches as they had done at Attu.

Consequently, the landings scheduled for the next morning were not canceled or altered. Aerial reconnaissance, which might have revealed the true state of affairs, was hampered by adverse weather.

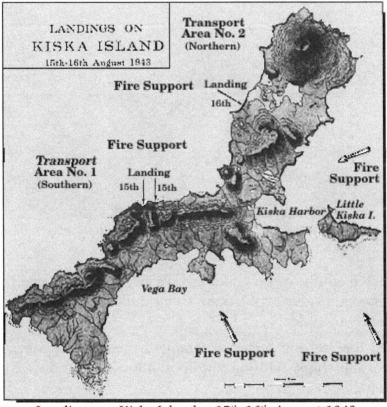

Landings on Kiska Island -- 15th-16th August 1943

At 2200 the minesweepers proceeded to the northern transport area and swept it, after which the transports involved in the demonstration on the southern side of the island came in and took up their positions. Special Service Force units landed at 0110 on the 16th. All assault waves, less Canadians, had been landed by 0800 without opposition. An hour later 3,100 troops were ashore. By noon Ranger Hill had bee occupied and indications of recent Japanese evacuation had been found. A few antipersonnel mines were located on the northern beaches.

Landing operations at Kiska, 15 August 1943

In the south, meanwhile, patrols began to find even more widespread evidence of Japanese evacuation within the past ten days or two weeks.

On the 16th the same prearranged fires were delivered by supporting ships, with ammunition allowances reduced by 50 per cent.

By 1600 on D plus 1 day, patrols reached the Gertrude Cove area, supposedly one of the enemy's most strongly held areas. It, too, was unoccupied. The Canadian troops had now landed on the northern beaches, making a total of about 7,000 men in that sector. Before the close of the day, many batteries of artillery were put ashore at all beaches. Aerial reconnaissance, to ascertain the position of the enemy, continued to be ineffective because of bad weather.

The next day further evidence of hasty abandonment was found. Little Kiska had apparently been evacuated about ten days earlier. Since there was no indication of the presence of the enemy, Commander Attack Force (Admiral Rockwell) relieved congestion at the beaches by ordering some transports to re-embark heavy equipment and proceed to more favorable anchorages near Kiska Harbor and Gertrude Cove. He had already released the *Tennessee, Idaho,* and screen to return to Adak.

LSTs unloading on Kiska after the landings

At 0244, 18 August, it was learned that the *Abner Read* had been severely damaged by an underwater explosion. While reversing course at five knots, the ship had her fantail blown off, probably by a mine. The vessel was able to proceed to Adak in tow of the *Ute,* but 61 personnel were listed as missing and 26 were injured.

By 0800 on the 18th enemy contacts ashore were still negative, although 26 casualties had been caused by mistaken identity in the heavy fog. Throughout the next few days, unloading, patrolling afloat and ashore, and other activities incident to the landing continued without hostile interference, and numerous ships were detached to return to base. At 1150, 22 August, Commander North Pacific Force (Admiral Kinkaid) announced that the amphibious phase of the operation would be considered complete at 1400. At that time Commander Attack Force in the *Pennsylvania* departed for Adak with screen.

Evacuation of Kiska by the Japanese

It is believed that the main Japanese evacuation took place on or about 28 July. At that time our covering task groups were operating to the southward of Attu-Kiska and to the westward and northwestward of Attu. Search planes were scanning all suspect areas as diligently as weather allowed. Nevertheless, it seems that the actual evacuation ships were not sighted, unless they were picked up on 29 July. Contacts were, however, made with submarines which may have played a minor part. Surface contacts in the period were limited to the following:

10 July: Four small AKs attacked by Army and Navy air west of Attu. Two sunk and the others turned back.
23 July: Seven "ships" contacted by Catalina radar southwest of Attu.
25 July: Another AK sighted.
25-26 July: Radar contacts bombarded by our task groups. These contacts were probably phantoms.
27 July: One 200-foot AK and 16 barges seen in Kiska Harbor.
29 July: Seven "ships" contacted by Catalina radar northwest of Attu.
2 August: Only one barge and one small boat seen on the beach near the main camp. In the interim, photographic coverage had been prevented by weather.

Radio transmissions from Kiska ceased on the 27th. Prior to that date our attacking airmen had noted extensive demolitions and alterations in the defenses of the island. Antiaircraft fire had diminished, and after 28 July it virtually ceased, only a small detachment of the enemy remaining on the island to fire light weapons and thus delude our fliers and the observers on our bombarding vessels. This rear guard was probably evacuated by submarine.

The fact that antiaircraft fire continued, although sporadically and in reduced volume, proved that the Japanese still remained on the island. The destruction and alteration of installations revealed by air photos was readily interpreted as evidence of defensive preparations. The cumulative impression was bolstered at the eleventh hour by the report of Liberators which raided Paramushiru on 12 August that a considerable Japanese naval force was concentrated in the Kuriles. Our leaders were led to suspect that the enemy was not only ready and waiting but was going to make a serious naval effort to oppose our landing. Any doubts of enemy resistance were not compelling enough to result in advance reconnaissance of Kiska except from the air.

Later reports indicated that the Japanese began their attempts to evacuate the island on about 10 July. The light surface force which was charged with this duty turned back at least six times because the weather was not thick enough. On the 26th (Tokyo time) the rescue force was again cruising about, awaiting favorable weather, when the minelayer *Kunijiri* apparently collided with the light cruiser *Abukuma*, causing slight damage. The resultant confusion brought about a triple collision in the rear of the column which forced one unit to return to Paramushiru. Evidently the weather played no favorites in Aleutian naval operations.

On the 28th (Tokyo time) it was decided to make a dash for Kiska, since the weather had closed down. On the way in, one destroyer mistook Little Kiska for an American patrol vessel and launched several torpedoes. Later another destroyer bombarded the same target. Loading of evacuees was accomplished in two hours. Paramushiru was safely reached on the 31st.

Conclusion

With the departure of the last Japanese from Kiska, the Aleutians Campaign may be said to have ended. But there was no cessation of the arduous, unspectacular effort which had brought success after nearly 15 months. The bitter battle against he weather went on as usual. Bases still had to be completed, and air facilities had to be improved and expanded for operations against the Kuriles.

The anticlimactic character of the invasion of Kiska, while disappointing because our forces, well-prepared at last, were prevented from coming to grips with the enemy, was compensated by lives saved and lessons learned under conditions which were nearly those of combat. The withdrawal of the Japanese without a fight was unfortunate in one sense, however. It presented us with a false picture of what might be expected from the enemy when the odds were hopelessly against him. Instead of fighting to the death, as at Attu, he had faded into the fog without a struggle. But Attu, and not Kiska, was to be the pattern of the future.

CPSIA information can be obtained
at www.ICGtesting.com
Printed in the USA
LVHW081121030822
725063LV00014B/895